THE TERRY LECTURES

FREUD AND THE PROBLEM OF GOD

HANS KÜNG

FREUD

AND THE PROBLEM

OF GOD

ENLARGED EDITION

TRANSLATED BY EDWARD QUINN

NEW HAVEN AND LONDON
YALE UNIVERSITY PRESS

Published by arrangement with Doubleday, a division
of Bantam Doubleday Dell Publishing Group, Inc.

The new material for the enlarged edition was
translated by Caroline Murphy.

Designed by Sally Harris
and set in VIP Zapf International type.
Printed in the United States of America by
Vail-Ballou Press, Binghamton, New York.

Library of Congress Cataloging-in-Publication Data
Küng, Hans, 1928–
    [Freud und die Zukunft der Religion.   English]
    Freud and the problem of God /Hans Küng ;
translated by Edward Quinn.—Enl. ed.
        p.   cm.—(Terry lectures ; v. 41)
    Translation of: Freud und die Zukunft der Religion.
    Includes his work originally published under title:
Does God exist?
    Includes bibliographical references.
    1. Psychoanalysis and religion.   2. Freud, Sigmund,
1856–1939—Religion.   3. Atheism.   I. Küng, Hans,
1928–   Existiert Gott? 1979.   II. Title.   III. Series.
BF175.4.R44K86   1990
200'.1'9—dc20   89–29650   CIP

ISBN 0–300–04711–8 (alk. paper)
    0–300–04723–1 (pbk.: alk. paper)

The paper in this book meets the guidelines for
permanence and durability of the Committee on
Production Guidelines for Book Longevity of the
Council on Library Resources.

10   9   8   7   6   5   4   3   2   1

THE DWIGHT HARRINGTON TERRY FOUNDATION LECTURES ON RELIGION IN THE LIGHT OF SCIENCE AND PHILOSOPHY

The deed of gift declares that "the object of this foundation is not the promotion of scientific investigation and discovery, but rather the assimilation and interpretation of that which has been or shall be hereafter discovered, and its application to human welfare, especially by the building of the truths of science and philosophy into the structure of a broadened and purified religion. The founder believes that such a religion will greatly stimulate intelligent effort for the improvement of human conditions and the advancement of the race in strength and excellence of character. To this end it is desired that a series of lectures be given by men eminent in their respective departments, on ethics, the history of civilization and religion, biblical research, all sciences and branches of knowledge which have an important bearing on the subject, all the great laws of nature, especially of evolution . . . also such interpretations of literature and sociology as are in accord with the spirit of this foundation, to the end that the Christian spirit may be nurtured in the fullest light of the world's knowledge and that mankind may be helped to attain its highest possible welfare and happiness upon this earth." The present work constitutes the forty-first volume published on this foundation.

To the American Psychiatric Association
in gratitude

CONTENTS

PREFACE

I am deeply grateful to Yale University for this invitation and greatly honored to be asked to follow the distinguished figures who have delivered the famous Terry Lectures in past years, to enter as it were an apostolic succession which includes not only outstanding theologians like Paul Tillich and Reinhold Niebuhr, but also Carl Gustav Jung and Erich Fromm, who have dealt so effectively, from the psychological standpoint, with many themes that come very close to my own. It is out of respect for these men that I have chosen a topic on the borderline between psychology and theology: Freud and the Problem of God.

I shall try to deal with the subject openly and fairly and especially to avoid two mistakes:

1. The mistake of those—theologians in particular—who see in Freud only the atheist, materialist, and pan-sexualist. But I hope that Freudian specialists will not find fault with the treatment in my first and second lectures of the genesis of Freud's atheism and his understanding of the origin and essence of religion.

2. The mistake of those—psychologists in particular—who see in Freud only the psychologist, psychotherapist, and psychoanalyst. In the third and fourth lectures I hope to face squarely the question of Freud's atheism, distinguishing what is valuable from what is not in his critique of religion.

The patient reader will find that his questions are raised and dealt with in the appropriate place. We shall proceed slowly, step by step: from the exposition to the critique, from the critique to the critique of the critique. As Hegel shows, truth is not the beginning, the middle, or the end, but the whole. You may judge the whole at the end.

PREFACE TO THE
ENLARGED EDITION

The dialogue between psychiatry, psychotherapy, and psychoanalysis on the one hand and theology and religion on the other
presents us with far greater complexities than it did ten years
ago. First, there is the current explosion of religiousness all
over the world in every possible form (mythical, cultic, and
mystical; Christian, Indian, and Far Eastern; progressive and
conservative). This explosion belies the thesis that religion is
dying, but it is looked upon by psychologists and theologians
alike with mixed feelings. Second, theologians have begun to
take the criticism of religion by psychoanalysis, which found
its great proponent in Sigmund Freud, seriously—in the sense
both of dismantling false, regressive, repressive notions of God
and of erecting "purified," "liberating," "healing" ones. And
third, despite this evolution in the response of theologians,
religion continues to be relegated to a corner in the realm of
psychology, psychiatry, and often psychotherapy. In the everyday practice of psychiatrists and especially psychoanalysts, religion—unlike sexuality—plays a negligible role. A case of
"repression"?

In 1979 I delivered the D. H. Terry Lectures at Yale University
on the topic "Freud and the Problem of God." The publication
by Yale University Press of this material—which is identical
with the Freud chapter from *Existiert Gott? Antwort auf die
Gottesfrage der Neuzeit*, Munich, 1978 (*Does God Exist? An
Answer for Today*, New York, 1981)—revitalized for many
American psychiatrists the question of religion's role in psychiatric practice. To my great joy the American Psychiatric

Association awarded me the Oscar Pfister Prize at its annual meeting in Washington in May 1986. I used my acceptance speech as an opportunity to undertake a systematic investigation—predicated on my earlier writings about Freud—of the repression of religion in psychiatry, psychotherapy, and psychoanalysis. Over the past few years I have had numerous occasions to discuss this problem critically with colleagues in psychiatry and psychotherapy. I am particularly grateful in this regard to Dieter Blumer (Detroit), Edgar Draper (Jackson), Hans Heimann (Tübingen), Wolfgang Loch (Tübingen), and Walter Pöldinger (Basel).

It seemed appropriate when publishing a new edition of my Terry Lectures to include my Pfister acceptance speech. Thus, the reader is presented at once with the background and approaches to the dynamic relation between psychiatry, psychotherapy, and theology. The purpose of this book will be served if it succeeds in opening new channels of discourse between disciplines that often seem so far removed from each other.

Tübingen
January 1990

GOD

AN INFANTILE ILLUSION?

THE GENESIS OF
FREUD'S ATHEISM

1

The grandfather of Marxist atheism and of Freudian atheism is Ludwig Feuerbach, who was first a theologian, then a Hegelian, and finally an atheistic philosopher. After the failure of the political revolution of 1848, it was Feuerbach who prophesied another—successful—revolution, which would be speeded up by the natural sciences, the radical, corrosive natural sciences, especially chemistry. Although reactionary governments, with their limited range of vision, had not noticed the fact, the natural sciences had "long before dissolved the Christian world view in nitric acid."[1] The philosopher, himself drawn to the natural sciences but continually falling back on theology, insisted that philosophy should be linked no longer with theology but with the natural sciences. After a hymn of praise to Copernicus, the "first revolutionary of modern times,"[2] he recommended Jakob Moleschott's chemical study, *Lehre der Nahrungsmittel. Für das Volk (Theory of Foodstuffs. For the People)*. It was Moleschott, together with Carl Vogt and Ludwig Büchner among other young natural scientists, and supported by Feuerbach's philosophical criticism of religion and immortality, who brought a specifically *natural scientific* materialism to fruition in the nineteenth century.

Hegel's and Schelling's speculative, idealist philosophy of nature was finally superseded by exact, inductive research in laboratories. German idealism had played down the materialistic systems of Democritus and Lucretius in antiquity, of La Mettrie and Holbach at the time of the French Enlightenment, but these systems now found approval in Germany, particularly among natural scientists. And the tempestuous

1. L. Feuerbach, *Die Naturwissenschaft und die Revolution*, 1850, in E. Thies's edition of Feuerbach's works, to be completed in six volumes, vols 1–4, Frankfurt, 1975– , vol. 4, pp. 243–65. Quotation, pp. 253–54.
2. L. Feuerbach, ibid., pp. 249–50.

development of the natural sciences, together with their subsequent technicalization and industrialization in France, England, and Germany, seemed to confirm materialism at every stage. The attempt to produce a primary organic material (uric acid) from inorganic materials had already succeeded (F. Wöhler in 1828). Experiments on animals also proved the dependence of mental life on bodily functions.

In the year 1854—when Pius IX in Rome defined Mary's immaculate conception—an open conflict broke out at the thirty-first assembly of German natural scientists and doctors in Göttingen, a conflict which was not, however, on a high philosophical or scientific level. This was the famous "materialism controversy" between the medical specialist Rudolph Wagner, working in the field of anatomy and physiology, and the physiologist Carl Vogt. Wagner wanted to defend, by philosophical and theological arguments, the descent of all men from a single pair of human beings and also the existence of a special, invisible, weightless "soul substance" against recent physiological theories.[3] When attacked, Vogt sharply discounted the traditional conception under the heading: "Blind Faith and Science,"[4] assuming on the contrary that there were several original human couples and comparing the relationship between brain and thought to that between liver and bile or between kidneys and urine. A confrontation of this kind— with obscurities, exaggerations, downright errors, and even coarse language on both sides—would scarcely be possible in a debate today. But who was right here?

---

3. R. Wagner, *Menschenschöpfung und Seelensubstanz. Ein anthropologischer Vortrag, gehalten in der ersten öffentlichen Sitzung der 31. Versammlung deutscher Naturforscher und Ärzte zu Göttingen am 18. September 1854*, Göttingen, 1854; cf. also the same author, *Über Wissen und Glauben mit besonderer Beziehung auf die Zukunft der Seelen*, Göttingen, 1854.

4. C. Vogt, *Köhlerglaube und Wissenschaft*, Giessen, 1854.

For the general public at that time the materialists had won the battle. After the controversy it was clear that religious persuasions had no place in questions of natural science or medicine. The interconnection of mechanical-natural laws had to be investigated to the very end without philosophical or theological reservations; there was no activity of consciousness without cerebral activity, no soul existing independently of the body; religion had nothing to do with science and—if it counted at all—was a private affair. Two years before the Göttingen discussion, the physiologist Moleschott had published *Der Kreislauf des Lebens (The Cycle of Life)*,[5] and a year after it, in 1855, Ludwig Büchner, a doctor, produced his *Kraft und Stoff (Force and Matter)*.[6] More than twenty editions of the letter made it the militant bible of the new scientific-materialistic world view. According to Büchner, the world as a whole, and also the human mind, are explained by the combined activity of materials and their forces. God is superfluous.

A year after the appearance of this book, on 6 May 1856, Sigismund Freud was born (he used the name "Sigmund" continuously after leaving school) in the small Catholic town of Freiberg in Moravia (now Czechoslovakia) where there were only 2 percent Protestants and about the same number of Jews.[7]

5. J. Moleschott, *Der Kreislauf des Lebens. Physiologische Antworten auf Liebigs Chemische Briefe*, Mainz, 1852.
6. L. Büchner, *Kraft und Stoff. Empirisch-naturphilosophische Studien*, Leipzig, 1855.
7. Most of Freud's works quoted here can be found in S. Freud, *Studienausgabe*, edited by A. Mitscherlich, A. Richards, and J. Strachey, vols 1–9, Frankfurt 1969–75. Texts not contained in that edition can be found in S. Freud, *Gesammelte Werke*, edited in chronological sequence by A. Freud and others, vols 1–18, Frankfurt, 1960–68. Basic for Freud's biography in his own "Selbstdarstellung" in *Gesammelte Werke* 14:31–96; see also his postscript ("Nachschrift") to this work, written in 1935, in *Gesammelte Werke* 16:29–34.
(Except where otherwise indicated all quotations in the present translation

From Natural Scientist to Atheist

Leaving Darwin aside for the time being, it was mainly the epoch-making progress of the two basic medical sciences of anatomy and physiology (including pathology) that favored a kind of *medical materialism*. Only a decade after the materialism controversy—during which time the family of the wool merchant Jakob Freud, with the four-year-old Sigmund, had moved to Vienna on account of business difficulties and continued in very straitened circumstances—Feuerbach, in one of his last works, *Über Spiritualismus und Materialismus (On Spiritualism and Materialism)* praised—of all people—the reformer Martin Luther, because the latter had allowed his son Paul to study medicine and so to be in a position to deny the immortality of the soul. The Reformation is thus seen as the beginning of German materialism. For Feuerbach, at any rate, it was clear at this time that the medical man was by nature a materialist.[8]

In fact, medicine in particular was of the greatest importance for materialistic atheism in the second half of the nineteenth century. At the time this atheism was not confined to the Marxist or non-Marxist workers' movement but was found primarily among the "enlightened" bourgeoisie, who had become increasingly estranged from both the Church and Christianity. From Feuerbach, therefore, the way led not only

---

will be taken from the *Standard Edition of the Complete Psychological Works of Sigmund Freud* in twenty-four volumes, from 1953 onward, published by the Hogarth Press and the Institute of Psycho-Analysis, London/Clarke Irwin and Co., Toronto. References to this edition will be indicated by *S.E.*, followed by volume, date, and page. "An Autobiographical Study" is in vol. 20, 1959, pp. 2–70, followed by "Postscript," pp. 71–74.—TRANS.

8. L. Feuerbach, *Über Spiritualismus und Materialismus, besonders in Beziehung auf die Willensfreiheit*, in *Sämtliche Werke*, Leipzig, 1846–66, 10:37–204. Quotation, p. 119.

to the Weltanschauung of dialectical materialism (Engels, incidentally, opposed Büchner's mechanistic, undialectical materialism); it led also—in fact, *via* mechanistic or even materialistic medicine—to Sigmund Freud's psychoanalysis. Quite apart from all this was the fact that Feuerbach upheld the fundamental significance of human sexuality and openly denounced idealistic-spiritualistic psychology and the prudery that came with it. This too contributed substantially to the breakdown of the considerable inhibitions preventing the scientific and medical investigation of sexuality.

According to Ernest Jones, a student of Freud and author of a monumental three-volume biography, running to more than fifteen hundred pages, the boy "grew up devoid of any belief in a God or Immortality, and does not appear to have felt the need of it."[9] This is a surprisingly sweeping statement, and one for which Jones, who sometimes goes on at great length about the most trivial details concerning his hero, can produce no evidence. In fact all that he says of the young Freud's attitude to religion proves the opposite: "Freud himself was certainly conversant with all Jewish customs and festivals."[10]

9. Ernest Jones, *Sigmund Freud. Life and Work*, Hogarth Press, London/Clarke Irwin, Toronto, three volumes published from 1953 onward. Editions used here are vol. 1, 1956; vol. 2, 1958; vol. 3, 1957. The quotation is from 1:22; cf. also 3:372–73.

On recent psychological and theological discussion of Freud cf. the following monographs: W. G. Cole, *Sex in Christianity and Psycho-Analysis*, London, 1956; J. Scharfenberg, *S. Freud und seine Religionskritik als Herausforderung für den christlichen Glauben*, 2d ed., Göttingen, 1970; the same author, *Religion zwischen Wahn und Wirklichkeit. Gesammelte Beiträge zur Korrelation von Theologie und Psychoanalyse*, Hamburg, 1972; A. Plé, *Freud et la religion*, Paris, 1968; P. Homans, *Theology after Freud. An Interpretative Inquiry*, New York, 1970.

Informative symposia on the subject include P. Homans (ed.), *The Dialogue between Theology and Philosophy*, Chicago, 1968; H. Zahrnt (ed.), *Jesus und Freud. Ein Symposion von Psychoanalytikern und Theologen*, Munich, 1972, with contributions by the psychoanalysts T. Brocher, A. Görres, M. Hirsch, and E. Wiesenhütter, and the theologians H. Fries and J. Scharfenberg.

Sigmund's father, Jakob Freud, a patriarchal figure, had been educated as an Orthodox Jew and, despite his liberal, aloof attitude to Jewish tradition, he was never converted to Christianity, unlike Karl Marx's father. When he was seventy-five years old he gave his son a Bible for his thirty-fifth birthday, with an inscription in Hebrew:

My dear Son

It was in the seventh year of your age that the spirit of God began to move you to learning. I would say the spirit of God speaketh to you: "Read in My book; there will be opened to thee sources of knowledge of the intellect." It is the Book of Books; it is the well that wise men have digged and from which lawgivers have drawn the waters of their knowledge.

Thou hast seen in this Book the vision of the Almighty, thou hast heard willingly, thou hast done and hast tried to fly high upon the wings of the Holy Spirit. Since then I have preserved the same Bible. Now, on your thirty-fifth birthday I have brought it out from its retirement and I send it to you as a token of love from your old father.[11]

Freud's mother called down the blessing of the Almighty on her son when he set up in practice, but Jones implies only that she "preserved some belief in the Deity."[12] Nevertheless it was

---

There are surveys of the discussion by K. Birk, *Sigmund Freud und die Religion*, Münsterschwarzach, 1970, and E. Wiesenhütter, *Freud und seine Kritiker*, Darmstadt, 1974.

Among recent helpful interpretations of Freudian thinking may be mentioned P. Ricoeur, *De l'interprétation. Essai sur Freud*, Paris, 1964; W. Loch, *Zur Theorie, Technik und Therapie der Psychoanalyse*, Frankfurt, 1972; A. Mitscherlich, *Der Kampf um die Erinnerung. Psychoanalyse für fortgeschrittene Anfänger*, Munich, 1975.

10. E. Jones, *Sigmund Freud* 1:21; cf. also vol. 1, chap. 2, "Boyhood and Adolescence" and vol. 3, chap. 13, "Religion."

11. Quoted in E. Jones, *Sigmund Freud* 1:21–22.

12. Ibid. 1:22.

she who instructed him in the Jewish faith. Such instruction, of course, could be of very dubious value, as is clear from Freud's later recollection:

> When I was six years old and was given my first lessons by my mother, I was expected to believe that we were all made of earth and must therefore return to earth. This did not suit me and I expressed doubts of the doctrine. My mother thereupon rubbed the palms of her hands together—just as she did in making dumplings, except that there was no dough between them—and showed me the blackish scales of *epidermis* produced by the friction as a proof that we were made of earth.[13]

In any case Freud himself admits that reading the Bible had made a strong impression on him as a young man: "My deep engrossment in the Bible story (almost as soon as I had learnt the art of reading), had, as I recognized much later, an enduring effect on the direction of my interest."[14] Professor Hammerschlag, who had taught him biblical history and Hebrew, remained throughout his life the most important of his older friends and one of the few "of whom Freud has no word whatever of criticism, and Freud was not sparing in this."[15]

It is unlikely, however, that present-day psychoanalysts will now be able to find out how far experiences in early childhood and the very complicated family relationships influenced the religious attitude of the boy Sigmund. It should be observed

---

13. S. Freud, *Die Traumdeutung* in *Studienausgabe* 2:215 (*The Interpretation of Dreams* in *S.E.*4 [1953]:205).

14. S. Freud, "Selbstdarstellung" in I. Grubrich-Simitis (ed.), *Schriften zur Geschichte der Psychoanalyse*, Frankfurt, 1971, p. 40. This sentence is lacking in the first edition of the "Selbstdarstellung" of 1925 (*Gesammelte Werke* 14:34) and was added only in 1935. ("An Autobiographical Study" in *S.E.* 20 [1959]: 8.)

15. E. Jones, *Sigmund Freud* 1:183.

that, after the death of his first wife, by whom he had two
children, Freud's father, Jakob Freud, forty years old and already a grandfather, married a Jewess who was not yet twenty.
A year later she brought Sigmund into the world as the first of
her eight children. Freud was thus an uncle from his birth
onward and his playmate, almost the same age and the
stronger of the two, was his nephew, son of his half brother
Emanuel and grandson of Jakob. Forty years later, after the
death of his father, Freud's unsparing self-analysis revealed the
peak of a neurosis: an unconscious jealousy of and aversion to
his father, who personified for him authority, refusal, and
compulsion, and at the same time a passion for his youthful
mother: in a word, what he called an Oedipus complex. From
then on, in order to prevent further children, he rigorously
avoided all sexual activity. This fact led not a few of his critics
to attribute his evaluation of sexuality to "sexual congestion."[16]
In any case he attributed his unshakable self-confidence, his
inner security, to his relationship with his mother: "If a man
has been his mother's undisputed darling he retains throughout life the triumphant feeling, the confidence in success,
which not seldom brings actual success along with it."[17]

Two kinds of "antireligious" experiences—like his aversion
to music—made a deep impression on Freud at an early age:
his experiences of ritualism and his experience of anti-
Semitism.

Experiences with Catholic *ritualism.* The old nanny who
looked after him during his earliest years was efficient and
strict, a Czech Catholic who implanted in the small boy
Catholic ideas of heaven and hell, and probably also of redemp-

16. Cf. E. Wiesenhütter, *Freud und seine Kritiker*, pp. 31–35.
17. S. Freud, "Eine Kindheitserinnerung aus 'Dichtung und Wahrheit' " in
Gesammelte Werke 12:26. ("A Childhood Recollection from *Dichtung und
Wahrheit*" in *S.E.* 17 [1955]:145–56. Quotation p. 156.)

tion and resurrection. She used to take him with her to Mass in the Catholic Church. At home afterward he would imitate the liturgical gestures, preach and explain "God's doings."[18] Could this have been the source of Freud's later aversion to Christian ceremonies and doctrines? At any rate it cannot be accidental that his first essay on religion, in 1907, bore the title: "Obsessive Actions and Religious Practices."[19] There he describes obsessional neuroses as a "pathological counterpart of the formation of a religion," and religion itself as a "universal obsessional neurosis."[20]

Experiences with Catholic *anti-Semitism*. Freud considered himself a Jew and was proud of the fact. But he had to suffer for it, although he was quite clearly first in his class at his secondary school and rarely had to face questions there. As an outsider at primary and secondary school, his position was similar to that of Karl Marx. He had only a few non-Jewish friends; humiliations of all kinds at the hands of anti-Semitic "Christians" were his daily lot. He would have preferred to have been educated, like his nephew John, in the more liberal atmosphere of England. But he lost much of his respect for his father when he learned at the age of twelve that Jakob Freud had simply swallowed the insult when a boy had thrown his new fur cap into the mud and shouted, "Get off the pavement, Jew."[21] Such experiences unleashed in Freud feelings of hatred and revenge at an early date and made the Christian faith completely incredible to him. It was no better at the university:

18. Marie Bonaparte, Anna Freud, Ernst Kris (eds.), *Aus den Anfängen der Psychoanalyse*, London, 1950, p. 236.
19. S. Freud, "Zwangshandlungen und Religionsübungen" in *Studienausgabe* 7:11–21. ("Obsessive Actions and Religious Practices" in *S.E.* 9 [1959]: 115–27.)
20. Ibid. 7:21. (*S.E.* 9:126–27.)
21. S. Freud, *Die Traumdeutung* in *Studienausgabe* 2:208. (*The Interpretation of Dreams* in *S.E.* 4:197.)

"Above all, I found that I was expected to feel myself inferior and an alien because I was a Jew. I refused absolutely to do the first of these things."[22] He was sixty-nine when he recorded this in his autobiography.

Nevertheless, these negative experiences with religion, however much they discredit Christianity, need not have shaken Freud's Jewish faith in God. How did this come about?

When he went to the university at the age of seventeen, Freud chose his calling only after some hesitation and certainly without regard to economic considerations. Although he had no particular inclination for it, he finally decided to become a doctor. According to his own later admission, this was the result not of a "craving to help suffering humanity," but of his "need to understand something of the riddles of the world in which we live and perhaps even to contribute something to their solution." Desire for knowledge, then, was the decisive factor. "The most hopeful means of achieving this end seemed to be to enroll myself in the medical faculty; but even after that I experimented—unsuccessfully—with zoology and chemistry, till at last, under the influence of Brücke, who carried more weight with me than anyone else in my whole life, I settled down to physiology, though in those days it was too narrowly restricted to histology."[23] Here he found men whom he "could respect and take as models."[24]

Thus Freud too had found his "second father." What Hegel had been for Feuerbach in Berlin, Brücke was in Vienna for Freud.

22. S. Freud, "Selbstdarstellung" in *Gesammelte Werke* 14:34. ("An Autobiographical Study" in *S.E.* 20:9.)

23. S. Freud, "Nachwort zur 'Frage der Laienanalyse' " in *Gesammelte Werke* 14:290. ("The Question of Lay Analysis. Postscript" in *S.E.* 20 [1959]:253.)

24. S. Freud, "Selbstdarstellung" in *Gesammelte Werke* 14:35. ("An Autobiographical Study" in *S.E.* 20 [1959]:9.)

At the same time he found himself among the main proponents of the very successful physical, *mechanistic* physiology, in the school of medicine, led by Helmholtz, that had emerged from a club of young physicists and physiologists in Berlin in the 1840s. They had been for the most part students of the great physiologist Johannes Müller and afterward they became lifelong friends, exercising an influence on the research of the next twenty or thirty years far beyond Germany. The group included Hermann Helmholtz, Emil Du Bois-Reymond, Carl Ludwig, and Ernst Brücke himself, a model of the disciplined, incorruptible, and serious natural scientist. Freud remained in Brücke's institute for six years and even then was reluctant to leave it.

Helmholtz, at one and the same time physicist, mathematician, and biologist—"one of my idols," said Freud in 1883[25]—at the age of twenty-six had helped to obtain recognition for the law of the conservation of energy, which had been discovered in 1842 by the doctor Robert Mayer and then given precise expression in a universal formula: the sum total of energy remains constant in any isolated system, no matter what changes take place in the individual energy components (mechanical, electrical, radiant, chemical). This law of conservation (the first law of thermodynamics), made it possible to assume a unity of all natural forces. Together with the law of entropy (heat can never be changed back completely into energy), it is the most fundamental of all laws of nature. It was only now that the mechanistic theory of the human body, supported by Descartes, was also able to exercise its full influence—but, as earlier with La Mettrie, at the expense of the human mind. The human organism, like inorganic nature,

25. S. Freud, in a letter to his fiancée, Martha Bernays, quoted by E. Jones, *Sigmund Freud* 1:45.

had to be understood from the interplay and transformation of physico-chemical forces or forms of energy. Helmholtz—who was, incidentally, also the inventor of a lens to focus the vessels of the retina (ophthalmoscope) and the author of a wide-ranging work on acoustics (embracing physics, physiology, psychology, and aesthetics)—succeeded in measuring the velocity of transmission of stimuli in the nerve fibres.

As early as 1842 Du Bois-Reymond, who carried out research into animal electricity in muscles and nerves, had written: "Brücke and I pledged a solemn oath to put into effect this truth: 'No other forces than the common physical and chemical ones are active within the organism. In those cases which cannot at the time be explained by these forces one has either to find the specific way or form of their action by means of the physical-mathematical method or to assume new forces equal in dignity to the chemical-physical forces inherent in matter, reducible to the force of attraction and repulsion.' "[26] In this way physicalist physiology got rid of the idealist philosophy of nature (*Naturphilosophie*) completely. And it eliminated all traces of the "vitalism" of the Aristotelian and Scholastic tradition, which assumed that organisms had been endowed by the Creator with immaterial factors—substantial forms, ends, purposes (entelechies)—and therefore with higher roles and ultimate objectives. What was now favored was a purely causal, deterministic explanation in the light of chemical-physical factors (that is, an explanation that would resemble artificial production of uric acid, already mentioned [p. 4]).

As Freud would say later, psychoanalysis too "derives all mental processes . . . from the interplay of forces which assist or inhibit one another, combine with one another, enter into

26. Ibid.

compromises with one another, etc."[27] Dispensing with an anatomical basis, Freud applied the principles of this physicalist-physiological science empirically to clinically observed psychological processes, the human psyche being understood as a kind of machine, as a "mental appliance." "Psychic energy" (energic cathexis and counter-cathexis, influx and discharge of energy, excitation, tension and displacement, and so on) thus became one of Freud's main concepts. In connection with the analysis of dreams as wish-fulfillment he was indeed able to introduce once more the terms *end, objective,* and *purpose*; but he did not abandon the deterministic assumptions which he regarded as equally valid for psychological and physical phenomena. For him, then, what appear to be the most obscure and fortuitous mental phenomena are wholly within the world of sense and wholly determined.

It is understandable that many people now saw the universal panacea for all the sufferings of the time in natural science and not in religion, politics, or philosophy. A method of investigation was turned into a world view; people "believed" in it. Freud also had an infinite reverence for this science as personified by his teacher Brücke and his assistants. He too "believed" in it. In any case, for him it meant the transition to atheism, if not for a time even to radical materialism, which, however, eminent scholars like Du Bois-Reymond and probably also Brücke rejected. But there is no direct evidence of this transition in Freud's own writings. This is odd. Freud, who otherwise relates the most intimate details of his life, does not say a word about this transition to atheism. Did he perhaps resist it? If we want to understand Freud's critique of religion,

27. S. Freud, "Psychoanalyse" in *Gesammelte Werke* 14:301. ("Psycho-Analysis" in *S.E.* 20 [1959]:265.)

we must go further back and trace more precisely his path to psychoanalysis.

From Physiology to Psychology

Since Freud did not feel drawn to practical work as a doctor either before or after his examinations (he graduated as a doctor in 1881), he continued his scientific research and laboratory work. The object of his investigations at this time was the spinal cord of one of the lowest forms of fish. His theoretical work in the physiological institute did not, of course, provide him with an adequate livelihood. Brücke therefore advised him to take up medical practice. For better or worse, from 1882 Freud worked in various departments of the Vienna General Hospital, especially in neuropathology, with the famous psychiatrist Meynert. But theory continued to be his main interest. While working intermittently at the laboratory of cerebral anatomy and at the children's clinic, he extended his investigations from animal nerve cells and nerve fibres to the human central nervous system. Right up to the 1890s he published a whole series of works including, in 1891, the most important of his neurological studies, on the subject of brain paralysis in children.[28]

He now obtained what he had sought for so long. From 1885 he was a nonsalaried teacher (*Privatdozent*) of neuropathology at the University of Vienna. The following year, at the age of thirty, he finally entered private practice as a specialist in nervous disorders. The opening took place on Easter Sunday, of all days—an "act of defiance" recalling the Easter feasts with his Catholic nanny, to whom he later ascribed a large part of

28. S. Freud, "Klinische Studie über die halbseitige Cerebrallähmung von Kindern" (1891) in *Beiträge zur Kinderheilkunde*, edited by M. Kassowitz, no. 3, Vienna, 1891.

his pyschological difficulties?[29] However that may be, after four years delay and almost daily correspondence with his distant fiancée (more than nine hundred love letters), Freud was now finally able to marry. Martha Bernays was from a well-known Jewish family in Hamburg, who, however, were not at all happy about a marriage with the impecunious and professionally not very successful, and even "pagan," Freud. Freud had to put up with a Jewish marriage rite and to learn the Hebrew texts, despite his life-long horror of ceremonies— particularly religious ceremonies. Under his influence, however, his wife gave up Orthodox Jewish customs, although she never denied her family's Jewishness. It was a happy marriage; it bore fruit in three sons and two daughters and formed for Freud a strong counterbalance to the unceasing difficulties in his profession.

There was certainly no lack of these. The anti-Semitic attitude prevailing in Vienna, Freud's glaring failure (afterward passed over in silence) in the matter of the medicinal use of cocaine, finally the increasingly widespread prejudices of his professional colleagues against Freud's unusual discoveries in connection with hysteria and hypnosis (regarded in Vienna as a priori "unserious" themes, even as "inauthentic" phenomena)—all these formed unsurmountable obstacles in the way of a call to an official teaching post at the university. Shortly before the opening of his private practice, Brücke had enabled him to obtain a travel scholarship to go to the "Mecca of neurology," the Paris nerve clinic under the great Jean Martin Charcot. Here he began to take an interest in hysteria (among men as well) and in hypnosis (as a healing method), the first beginnings of his *investigation of the soul*, the turning from neurology to psychopathology. When he returned to

29. Cf. E. Jones, *Sigmund Freud* 1:158, 358.

Vienna, Freud met with opposition: hysteria in men, hysterical paralyses produced by hypnotic suggestion? No one wanted to believe this. But he began gradually to expand his discoveries into a systematic method of research.

In 1889 Freud learned from specialists in Nancy (Liebault, Bernheim), the technique of hypnotic suggestion, but in practice this did not satisfy him any more than experiments with electrotherapy. It was only the experiences of his older medical friend Josef Breuer with an intelligent young woman suffering from hysteria (the famous case of Fräulein Anna O = Bertha Pappenheim), which brought him further. He began to see and to treat hysteria and its symptoms as products of emotional shocks (traumas). The patient had forgotten, "repressed," them; now he had to recall them under hypnotic suggestion in order to "abreact" instead of repressing them. Thus the patient could gradually be healed of the unconscious stimulus (later called a "complex"), which had remained untreated, and of his morbid symptoms; but this could not happen without a certain "transference-love" for the doctor (not admitted by Breuer at the time). Breuer and Freud called this the *method of catharsis* (purification).[30]

Freud's transition from physiology to psychology now became increasingly decisive. It was first given shape in 1895 in his "Project of a Psychology"[31] (which was made known only to Wilhelm Fliess, a Berlin doctor), a description of psychological processes, but still in purely physiological terminology (as quantifiable states of the nerve-cells or *neurons*). Five years

30. S. Freud and J. Breuer, *Studien über Hysterie* (1895) in *Gesammelte Werke* 1:75–312. (*Studies on Hysteria, S.E.* 2 [1955].)

31. S. Freud, "Entwurf einer Psychologie" (1895), first published 1950 in M. Bonaparte, A. Freud, and E. Kris (eds.), *Aus den Anfängen der Psychoanalyse*, London, 1950, pp. 371–466. Cf. W. Salber, *Entwicklungen der Psychologie Freuds*, vol. 1, Bonn, 1973, especially pp. 106–33.

later, in *The Interpretation of Dreams*, he still described psychological processes with the aid of numerous individual features and structural characteristics from physiology, but without proving the existence of a physical-physiological basis of the clinically observed psychological processes. Freud now increasingly gave a psychological meaning to physiological expressions. For there is a parallelism and interaction between physiological and psychological processes, which of course had not hitherto been explained.

How did Freud reach this stage? "I was always open to the ideas of G. T. Fechner and have followed that thinker on many important points," wrote Freud in his autobiography.[32] In fact, in his basic psychological ideas, Freud leaned heavily on Fechner, the founder of experimental psychology (who himself derived many of his ideas from the philosopher and psychologist J. F. Gerbart).[33] Fechner had at that time produced the only important counter-proposal by a natural scientist against the materialism of Moleschott, Vogt, and Büchner, and he exercised a powerful influence on Freud's teachers—both Brücke the physiologist and Meynert the psychiatrist.

But the more independently Freud made use of the cathartic method in theory and practice, the more he found himself on a different path, a revolutionary against the traditional dogmas of medicine. He had an unexpected experience, but one which was soon to be confirmed, that what lies behind the manifestations of neurosis are not just any kind of emotional stirrings; rather, as a rule present or former sexual disturbances are secretly at work (not so much actual seductions as sexual fantasies—a fact he established only at a later date). Freud went on, consistently, to investigate the sexual life of

32. S. Freud, "Selbstdarstellung" in *Gesammelte Werke* 14:86. ("An Autobiographical Study" in *S.E.* 20 [1959]:59.)
33. G. T. Fechner, *Elemente der Psychophysik*, 2 vols., Leipzig, 1860.

neurotics—which again hardly made his position in Vienna any easier. The consequences included the loss of a number of patients, the universal criticism of his professional colleagues, and in particular a break in his twenty-year-old friendship with Breuer (1895), now compensated by his intense friendship with the abovementioned Wilhelm Fliess.

The Realm of Concealed Wishes

Very much later Freud was to make a critical analysis of religion, which would render him even more suspect in Catholic Vienna. He would ask about the source of the inner strength of religious ideas. And his answer would be that they "are not precipitates of experiences or end results of our thinking," but "illusions, fulfilments of the oldest, strongest and most urgent wishes of mankind. The secret of their strength lies in the strength of those wishes."[34] If we are not to misunderstand this basic answer of Freud to the question about the essence of religion, we must keep clearly in mind his new insights into the human psyche and also into the meaning of wishing. It is not only or even primarily a question of conscious wishes, of human consciousness. We are now coming close to what constitutes psychoanalysis.

Freud had discovered the dynamism of the human psyche, the interplay of forces, especially of that mental stratum, often scarcely noticed and by some people completely denied, which is not accessible to direct knowledge: the *unconscious*, which is at first completely dark and—by comparison with conscious mental life—apparently unaccountable. His main insight was that all psychical activity is at first unconscious. Here we have

34. S. Freud, *Die Zukunft einer Illusion* in *Studienausgabe* 9:135–89; quotation, p. 164. (*The Future of an Illusion* in *S.E.* 21 [1961]:5–56. Quotation p. 30.)

the "primary" psychic processes; the conscious processes, on the other hand, are "secondary." Freud's epoch-making achievement was, after infinite pains, to make the *unconscious*—which hitherto, in Romanticism, for instance, had been more suspected than investigated—the object of *methodical scientific exploration*, distinguishing between the preconscious and the unconscious properly so called, and very much later between different agencies or systems of the psyche: ego, id, superego.

Freud discovered that in the normal case unconscious, repulsive instinctual impulses are rejected by consciousness, by the ego, after a more or less intense conflict; the energy is withdrawn or discharged. But in certain cases these instinctual impulses are not even brought into the conflict. Rejected by the ego from the outset through a primary defensive mechanism, they are shifted—repressed—into the unconscious, with their full energy cathexis, the sum total of energy remaining constant. This results in substitute satisfaction in the form of dreams or even bodily neurotic systems.

The task of therapy, therefore, is not simply to abreact the traumatic or neurotic affects, but to expose them as repressions. They are to be raised up into consciousness and, as a result of the collaboration of patient and therapist, to be replaced by judgments, which may mean the acceptance or rejection of the previously rejected instinctual impulses. Thus Freud had found his different path. It was to lead to the cure of mental illnesses by laying bare unconscious, untreated traumatic experiences and affects; but this was no longer to be brought about through hypnotic exploration ("reconnoitering" the psyche in a state of hypnosis), which was often unsuccessful, nor, as Freud had first attempted, through pressure and insistent interrogation on the part of the therapist, but rather as a result of *the patient's own "free association."* This means that the patient is to say with complete honesty everything—really everything—that comes into his mind at the moment, while avoiding any deliberate objectives. What is repressed can thus be brought into consciousness despite the resistance of the latter. The patient then comes to know himself to the very depths of his existence. Freud gave the new procedure of investigation and cure the name of *psychoanalysis*.

Freud, however, had recognized that the patient's resistance to admitting these things into consciousness could be laid bare and overcome only if the analyst had mastered that particular kind of interpretation, which has to be acquired, which leaves to the patient the course of the analysis and the arrangement of the material. There was one thing Breuer had not understood and consequently not admitted—the factor of "transference," the positive or negative emotional relationship of the patient to the analyst, which arises without the latter's wish, and also the reverse phenomenon of the "counter-transference" of the analyst on to the patient. But for Freud transference now becomes the decisive turning point of the therapeutic process. It makes possible both the doctor's influence and the patient's resistance. Something emerges which was later called a "working agreement" or "therapeutic alliance." Only in this way—on the doctor, so to speak, as the duplicate of a person formerly experienced—can the patient experience again his repressed positive or negative emotional relations to important persons in the past (especially parents, brothers, and sisters). Only in this way is it possible to catch sight of the unconscious structures and dynamic forces at work here and so to lay bare, interpret, and formulate the unconscious motivations. Only in this way is it possible to achieve a lasting transformation of the mental resources and the disappearance of the morbid symptoms, together with a deactivation of the transference. The patient ought to be able to love and work again. This, according to Freud, is the object of therapy.

But what is the best way to this goal? The main route of psychoanalysis, the *via regia*, the royal road into the dark realm of the unconscious, is the *interpretation of dreams*. What seems at first to be a pointless dream certainly has a meaning, if we look not simply at the conscious "manifest dream content," but at the preconscious "latent dream thoughts" which are processed in the dream. If we investigate these we find mainly traces left over from the person's waking life, "day's residues." Alongside these, however, there is often a very repulsive, formerly repressed wish impulse, which is what really shaped the dream and summoned up the energy for its production. It makes use of the day's residues as material, in order—when the repressive resistance of the ego is shut off during sleep—to press forward into consciousness with the aid of the dream. But, because of the dream censorship of the ego (the residue of the repressive resistance), the preconscious dream material must be changed, diminished, condensed, displaced, distorted, and finally dramatized. This is the process of "dream work." It leads to the typical "dream distortion" and permits it to be seen clearly as a substitute and compromise formation.

As early as 1895 Freud had discovered the element of meaning in the dream: "Dreams are wish fulfilments."[35] That is, dreams—like the neurotic symptoms which at first are equally unintelligible—are *disguised* fulfillments of a wish that is *repressed* and therefore needs interpretation. Repressed traumas can thus be analyzed and understood with the help of dreams. Or even with the help of the small slips and symptomatic actions of everyday life (slips of the tongue or pen; misreading or misplacing; forgetting resolutions, names, or experiences),

35. S. Freud, "Entwurf einer Psychologie," p. 424 (cf. n. 31, above.)

which are by no means accidental but bring to light unconscious processes, as Freud explained in 1904 in a book that was
the first of his to become popular, *The Psychopathology of
Everyday Life*. But the book which remains fundamental, and
which Freud always regarded as his most important, is *The
Interpretation of Dreams*, published, like Harnack's *Essence of
Christianity*, in the year of 1900,[36] and at first completely
ignored by the general public and destructively criticized in
specialist periodicals. It was hardly a good start for the "Father
of Psychoanalysis." In the course of six years only 351 copies of
this the most original and important work of Sigmund Freud
were sold. In the same year, 1900, three people attended his
course of lectures on dreams.

Nevertheless, from the standpoint of the understanding of
dreams, psychoanalysis no longer appeared to be merely an
auxiliary science to psychopathology. It also provided a starting
point for a more thorough understanding of the mental life of
the normal, healthy human being. With the aid of dream
interpretation in particular the analysis could penetrate to the
forgotten material of the years of childhood. While looking for
sexual conflict situations, from which repressions result, Freud
came in fact to the investigation of the earliest years of childhood, which, by no means sexually "innocent," proved to be
highly significant for the person's development as a whole. If
we do not want to misunderstand from the outset Freud's
theory of *infantile sexuality*, which seemed very shocking at the
time, we must know what he meant by the often misinter-
preted term *libido*. Libido (which is also to be found even in
children), is the energy of the sexual urges. It is not, however,
linked solely with the genital organs but represents a more

36. S. Freud, *Die Traumdeutung* (1900) in *Studienausgabe* II. (*The Interpretation of Dreams* in S.E. 4 and 5 [1953].)

comprehensive pleasure-seeking bodily function (sensuality in the widest sense of the term). It is common to both children and adults, normal and abnormal people, and thus includes also all merely tender or friendly feelings (all kinds of "love"). Why did he broaden the meaning of the term *sexuality* so much? For Freud it was only in this way that he found it possible to elaborate a comprehensive theory of sexuality—its wish fantasies (later the Oedipus complex in particular), its various early phases (auto-erotic, oral, anal, genital), its fixations at certain stages of development, its regressions to these stages in the event of repression, its sublimation or applicability for numerous cultural achievements.

These, then, are the two most important of Freud's scientific achievements: his theory of the unconscious and of the way it works (primary process, interpretation of dreams) and his theory of the libido (including infantile sexual life). In both these epoch-making discoveries Freud's self-analysis (undertaken systematically from 1897) played a decisive role. At the same time, as already mentioned, he discovered in himself an early childhood passion for his mother and jealousy of his father, which he looked on as a universally human characteristic, given expression at an early date in the myth of King Oedipus, who without knowing it had killed his father and married his mother.[37]

In 1905 Freud summed up the essentials of his surprising conclusions on human sexual life in *Three Essays on the Theory of Sexuality*,[38] a work whose later editions always appeared with corrections and additional material (from 1908 it included direct observation of children). Freud regarded it as his most important book after *The Interpretation of Dreams*. Fi-

37. Cf. E. Jones, *Sigmund Freud* 1:356–60.
38. S. Freud, *Drei Abhandlungen zur Sexualtheorie* (1905) in *Studienausgabe* 5:37–145. (*Three Essays on the Theory of Sexuality* in S.E. 7 [1954]:123–246.)

nally, in 1916 to 1917, he was able to produce his *Introductory Lectures on Psycho-Analysis*[39]—a large synthesis consisting of the three parts—"Parapraxes," "Dreams," and "General Theory of the Neuroses"—which was supplemented in 1933 by *New Introductory Lectures on Psycho-Analysis*.[40]

Freud now was no longer isolated as he had been during the decade after the separation from Breuer. In 1902 he had at last received the title of professor (*extraordinarius*), so important for medical men in Vienna, but it was only in 1920 that he became full professor. His students and comrades in arms now increasingly supported him—at first a small group in Vienna; then Eugen Bleuler, the great Swiss psychiatrist, and C. G. Jung, with whom Freud founded a psychoanalytical review, followed shortly by a second and third. Finally, in 1910, the International Psycho-Analytical Association was set up with a number of local groups and with Jung as its first president. In the previous year Freud and Jung, who were still being ostracized and vilified in Germany, had gone as visiting lecturers to Worcester, Massachusetts, and there met the Harvard neurologist J. J. Putnam and the philosopher William James. And when subsequently, after Bleuler, Jung and Alfred Adler also separated from Freud and founded their own schools of depth psychology, psychoanalysis had become sufficiently established in its theory, practice, and organization, so that Freud could get on not only with expanding the theoretical structure of psychoanalysis itself (with reference to the Oedipus complex, narcissism, the theory of instincts and its application to psychoses), but also with transferring its as-

39. Cf. S. Freud, *Vorlesungen zur Einführung in die Psychoanalyse* (1916–17) in *Studienausgabe* 1:33–445. (*Introductory Lectures on Psycho-Analysis* in *S.E.* 15 and 16 [1963].)

40. S. Freud, *Neue Folge der Vorlesungen zur Einführung in die Psychoanalyse* (1933) in *Studienausgabe* 1:446–608. (*New Introductory Lectures on Psycho-Analysis* in *S.E.* 22 [1964]:3–182.)

sumptions and conclusions to other varieties of emotional and mental events.

With the interpretation of dreams (and especially with the theory of the Oedipus complex), psychoanalysis had long before *crossed the frontiers of medicine.* And Freud himself, for whom psychoanalysis had become the whole content of his life, now showed how widely its application could be extended in a variety of greater and smaller works, including essays on a childhood memory of Leonardo da Vinci, delusion and dreams in Wilhelm Jensen's *Gradiva*, Michelangelo's Moses, a childhood recollection of Goethe from *Dichtung und Wahrheit*, and Dostoevsky and parricide. Psychoanalysis was now applied to literature and aesthetics, to mythology, folklore, and educational theory, to prehistory and the history of religion. It was no longer merely a therapeutic procedure, but an instrument of universal enlightenment.

After an unavoidably lengthy preparation, we have thus reached once again our proper theme, the theme which Freud too had reached at the end of his long road from cerebral anatomy and cerebral physiology, by way of psychopathology, to his new form of psychology (*metapsychology*). He was now ready to present his critique of religion.

Two questions have been continually kept alive by the different branches of the modern scientific study of religions, and these occupied Freud as well: what is the origin of religion and what is the nature of religion? The two questions are connected.

FREUD'S UNDERSTANDING OF
THE ORIGIN AND NATURE
OF RELIGION

2

What is the Source of Religion?

First of all we must glance at the historical background. For Freud the question of the origin of the different religions was quite obviously psychological in character. For Christian and Jewish *theologians* it had for centuries been a dogmatic question. The pagan religions were distortions, degenerations of the original pure revealed religion (with its primordial revelation), resulting from man's sin as described in the Bible. But for the rationalist "enlighteners" of the eighteenth century too—David Hume in England; Rousseau, Voltaire, and Diderot in France; Gotthold Ephraim Lessing in Germany—it was also a dogmatic question. The different religions were distortions and degenerations of the originally pure religion of reason, with its clear belief in God, freedom, and immortality, distortions brought about as a result of priestly inventions and popular customs. It was only with the rise of a *science of religion* in the nineteenth century that the question of the origin of religion became a historical, philological, ethnological, and psychological question. Even in classical Greece, of course, there had been an interest in the history of religions; but a science of religion as a specific field of study has existed only from the nineteenth century onward. In this field primitive religion itself became a problem.

Philologists of all kinds—Sinologists, Indologists, Iranists, Assyriologists, Egyptologists, Arabists, Germanists, classical philologists, as well as Old Testament and New Testament exegetes—were now concerned to bring out the numerous missing religious documents of the literate peoples and to throw light on the close connection between religion and language. By a comparative study of the ancient myths and fables German philologists like Jakob Grimm and Wilhelm Schwartz hoped to be able to reconstruct the primitive Germanic religion and even the oldest Indo-European religion. The myth-researcher Adolf Kuhn, who also drew on Indian sources, and F. Max Müller, the real founder of the "science of religion" (*Religionswissenschaft*), and responsible for the use of the term, both saw natural phenomena behind all myths and in accordance with this they arrived at the reconstruction of a poetic religion of nature. Does this represent the historical truth?

British *anthropologists* and *ethnologists*, however, in virtue of their philosophical tradition and cosmopolitan colonial interests during the rise of the Empire, took a different view. The earliest religion was not to be speculatively constructed in the light of ancient mythological traditions, but investigated empirically, on the spot, by direct study of the religions of the uncultured, illiterate ("primitive") peoples ("nature peoples"). Ethnology (anthropology) and the science of religion (history, phenomenology, psychology, and sociology of religion), could subsequently be separated in theory but scarcely in practice. People now—at the time of Darwin—wanted to see "evolution" everywhere.

"At the same time, the theories of Darwin, which were then of topical interest, strongly attracted me, for they held out hopes of an extraordinary advance in our understanding of the world."[1] This was how Freud at almost seventy described his schoolboy interests and his resolve to study medicine. Charles Darwin had in fact brought to fruition the idea of evolution, not only in biology and the natural sciences, but also, in an epoch-making fashion, in ethnology, the new science of religion and the history of religion. The theological scheme of a beginning on the heights, a pure monotheism and a paradisiac

---

1. S. Freud, "Selbstdarstellung" in *Gesammelte Werke* 14:34. ("An Autobiographical Study" in *S.E.* 20 [1959]:8.)

state of human perfection, as presupposed by the theory of degeneration, was replaced by a scientifically corrected scheme of a beginning in the depths, a primitive human state featuring an elemental belief in "powers" or spirits, which only gradually developed into something higher (theory of evolution).

The idea of evolution as such was not new. It had its starting points in Greek antiquity, in the work of Empedocles and Lucretius, and it was accepted, especially from Leibniz's time onward, into both German idealism and French positivism. Hegel and Comte in particular had prepared the way for it in their philosophies of history. The philosopher and sociologist Herbert Spencer, Darwin's English contemporary and the leading philosophical defender of evolutionism in the nineteenth century, had proclaimed, even before Darwin, development from lower to higher grades as the basic law of all reality and had made it the foundation of his "system of synthetic philosophy."[2] On the ethnological plane the theory of evolution was established by E. B. Tylor, specialist in cultural anthropology and first professor of the subject at Oxford.[3] Religion too, it was claimed, had developed in a straight line from the Stone Age up to the present time, uniformly throughout the same phases, in small steps, from lower to higher forms—naturally, at different paces in different areas. Thus all that needed to be done was to investigate the religion of the "primitive" nature-peoples and its survivals in later religions, and the earliest religion would be found.

From Tylor onward it was assumed that *animism* represented the first stage or—better—merely the threshold of reli-

2. H. Spencer, *The Principles of Psychology*, London, 1855; the same author, *First Principles*, London, 1862, which appeared as vol. 1 of *A System of Synthetic Philosophy*.

3. E. B. Tylor, *Primitive Culture. Researches into the Development of Mythology, Philosophy, Religion, Art and Customs*, 2 vols., London, 1871.

gion. It was understood as a belief, existing in a pure or hybrid form, in anthropomorphically conceived "souls" or, later, "spirits" (from the Latin *animi*, independently existing souls): a belief that everything is ensouled. Belief in souls or spirits was then followed by polytheistic belief in gods and finally monotheistic belief in one God. Wilhelm Wundt provided a psychological substructure for this view of the animistic origin of religion.[4] Later there were some who, with R. R. Marett in England, assumed a preliminary preanimistic stage.[5] *Preanimism* is here regarded as a minimal definition of religion, a stage at which man, before coming to believe in particular spirits, believes in a mysterious, supposedly impersonal animating force or power (Melanesian *mana*) in all things. On the one hand there is belief in the existence of souls in all things (*animism*), and on the other belief that there is life in all earthly things (*animatism*).

The Scotsman W. Robertson Smith, however, had brought out the fact that it was not so much belief in spirits or gods, but the sacred action, the rite, the cult, which was fundamental to religion.[6] For him, therefore, *totemism*, veneration of an animal as he had found it in a primitive Australian clan and as it had been known in all peoples, was the original religion. The clan regards itself as related to a particular totem, an animal, or, later, a plant or natural phenomenon, or even as descended from it (*totem* means kinship). The totem animal protects the group and may not be injured or killed. Members of the same totem group are not permitted to have sexual intercourse with one another, but only outside the group (*exogamy*). Thus the first ethical precepts follow from totemism: prohibition of

4. W. Wundt, *Völkerpsychologie. Eine Untersuchung der Entwicklungsgesetze von Sprache, Mythus und Sitte*, vol. 2, *Mythus und Religion*, Leipzig, 1905–09.
5. R. R. Marett, *The Threshold of Religion*, 2d ed., London, 1909, 1914.
6. W. Robertson Smith, *Lectures on the Religion of the Semites*, Edinburgh, 1898.

murder and of incest, according to Robertson Smith, the two prevailing *taboos* (a Polynesian word meaning "marked off," "prohibited," that is, "untouchable"). Once in the year the totem animal is ritually killed and devoured in order to renew the strength of the clan or tribe. From this quasi-sacramental totem-meal have emerged both the veneration of divine beings, at first in animal form, and also sacrifice.

According to the evolutionary scheme the life of the nature-peoples cannot be imagined as anything but primitive—gloomy and even, some have thought, almost without speech, communication taking place only by gestures and grunts. Consequently any cult at the level of animism or totemism can be no more than *magic* (or sorcery), consisting of actions and especially words which are, as it were, automatic in their effect and which are supposed to have a compelling influence on the powers of nature. It was thought that belief in spirits and gods, and therefore *religion* as a means of placating the powers of nature, developed only with the increasing awareness of the ineffectiveness of magic, especially in face of death. And finally, very much later, as a result of further corrections in attitude, rational, scientific thinking—*science*—emerged.

The famous triadic scheme of world history associated with Hegel and Comte now appears in another guise. Magic, religion, and science are now seen as stages in the evolutionary scheme of the history of religion. The theory was supported with an enormous amount of factual material by J. G. Frazer, the British ethnologist and investigator of religion, who under the influence of Robertson Smith and Wilhelm Mannhardt[7] distinguished between imitative and sympathetic magic.[8]

7. W. Mannhardt, *Der Baumkultus der Germanen und ihrer Nachbarstämme*, Berlin, 1875; the same author, *Antike Wald- und Feldkulte*, Berlin, 1877.
8. J. G. Frazer, *The Golden Bough. A Study in Comparative Religion*, 2 vols.,

It was precisely this *ethnological explanation of religion* and this evolutionary scheme of the early classical writers on the history of religion which Freud adopted. He was directly prompted to do this by C. G. Jung's comparative studies of religion and by his large work *Symbols of Transformation;*[9] but for his own part he relied especially on Robertson Smith, Frazer, and also Marett. Freud was at first concerned simply to corroborate from the history of religion the thesis he had put forward as early as 1907, that religious rites are similar to neurotic obsessive actions. This he did in four essays published as a book under the general title *Totem and Taboo* (1912).[10] Whether investigating the horror of incest (first essay), taboo prohibitions as a whole (second essay), animism and magic (third essay), or even totemism (fourth essay), he finds everywhere a similarity between the customs and religious attitudes of primitives, on the one hand, and the obsessive actions of his neurotic patients on the other, everywhere a survival of primitive mental life up to the present time. Nevertheless Freud now modifies his former provocative statement to the effect that religion is a universal obsessional neurosis. Despite any similarity between obsessional neurosis and religion, the former is in fact a distortion of the latter: "It might be maintained that a case of hysteria is a caricature of a work of art, that an obsessional neurosis is a caricature of a religion

London, 1890; the same author, *Totemism and Exogamy. A Treatise on Certain Early Forms of Superstition and Society*, 4 vols., London, 1910.

9. C. G. Jung, *Wandlungen und Symbole der Libido*, Vienna, 1912; 4th revised edition under the title *Symbole der Wandlung* (1952) in *Gesammelte Werke*, vol. 5, Zurich and Stuttgart, 1973. (English translation, *Symbols of Transformation*, translated from the 4th German edition, in *Collected Works*, vol. 5, published by Routledge and Kegan Paul, London/H. Wolff, New York, 1956.)

10. S. Freud, *Totem und Tabu. Einige Übereinstimmungen im Seelenleben der Wilden und Neurotiker* (1912–13) in *Studienausgabe* 9:287–444. (*Totem and Taboo in S.E.* 13 [1957]:1–161.)

and that a paranoic delusion is a caricature of a philosophical system."[11]

But Freud wanted to do more than simply draw attention to this similarity. He wanted to produce a *psychogenesis of religion*, the basic concept of which had been fixed in his mind from the outset: "I am reading thick books without being really interested in them since I already know the results; my instinct tells me that. But they have to slither their way through all the material on the subject."[12] Where had Freud obtained his results? From his total psychoanalytical view and his clinical experiences, which he put forward, after discussing different unsatisfying theories, to explain totemism.

In his observation of small children he had been particularly impressed by the fact that they like animals at first but begin to show fear of them at a later phase of development. If animal phobias of this kind are examined in children or even in those adults who have retained their childish phobias in a neurotic form, the reason is found to be a fear of one's own father, which however is projected on to the animal as a father symbol. Why? The child really wants to respect and love its father and yet fears him at the same time. This fear, however, is not consciously worked up but repressed by consciousness into the unconscious. It survives there and turns up again in a different form. An animal appears in place of the father. Yet the ambivalent feelings, both love and fear, are really directed toward the father; the animal merely replaces him as a substitute.

This psychoanalytical explanation Freud now applied to totem belief in the last of his four essays. Under the title of "The Return of Totemism in Childhood," he attempted to give

11. S. Freud, *Totem und Tabu* in *Studienausgabe* 9:363. (*Totem and Taboo* in *S.E.* 13 [1957]:72.
12. Quoted by E. Jones, *Sigmund Freud* 2:394.

a psychological explanation of religion. The same ambivalence of feelings can be observed in behavior toward totem animals: killing is prohibited, but the animal is sacrificed. The members of the totem group therefore behave toward the totem animals as children and neurotics do toward the animals they come across. For the former also the animal is a symbol for the father, more precisely a symbol for the primogenitor.

This means that behind totemism, this transitional stage even for more advanced peoples, what is secretly at work is nothing other than the Oedipus complex: attachment to the mother and death wish to the father, who is seen as a rival. And the very core of totemism—the totem meal in which annually, the totem animal as a sacred object is ritually killed and eaten, then mourned and finally celebrated by a feast—makes it clear that killing the father is the starting point of totemism and thus of the formation of religion as a whole.

Is it possible, however, to provide historical evidence of such a parricide? Freud appeals here to Darwin's "assumption" that human beings originally lived in packs or hordes (comparable to herds of deer), all the females being under the domination of a strong, brutal, jealous male. Freud later persisted in this view, which he had developed in *Totem and Taboo*, without correcting or amplifying it. He sums it up in his autobiography as follows:

> The father of the primal horde, since he was an unlimited despot, had seized all the women for himself; his sons, being dangerous to him as rivals, had been killed or driven away. One day, however, the sons came together and united to overwhelm, kill, and devour their father, who had been their enemy but also their ideal. After the deed they were unable to take over their heritage since they stood in one another's way. Under the influence of failure

and remorse they learned to come to an agreement among themselves; they banded themselves into a clan of brothers by the help of the ordinances of totemism, which aimed at preventing a repetition of such a deed, and they jointly undertook to forgo the possession of the women on whose account they had killed their father. They were then driven to finding strange women, and this was the origin of the exogamy which is so closely bound up with totemism. The totem meal was the festival commemorating the fearful deed from which sprang man's sense of guilt (or "original sin") and which was the beginning at once of social organization, of religion and of ethical restrictions.[13]

Thus religion is based entirely on the Oedipus complex of mankind as a whole.

For Freud this is the psychological explanation of the origin of religion. The formation of religion is built on the father complex and its ambivalence: "After the totem animal had ceased to serve as a substitute for him, the primal father, at once feared and hated, revered and envied, became the prototype of God himself. The son's rebelliousness and his affection for his father struggled against each other through a constant succession of compromises, which sought on the one hand to atone for the act of parricide and on the other to consolidate the advantage it had brought. This view of religion throws a particularly clear light upon the psychological basis of Christianity, in which, as we know, the ceremony of the totem meal still survives, with but little distortion, in the form of *Communion*."[14]

13. S. Freud, "Selbstdarstellung" in *Gesammelte Werke* 14:93 f. ("An Autobiographical Study" in *S.E.* 20:p. 68.)
14. Ibid. 14:94. (*S.E.* 20:68.)

Unlike Judaism, Christianity admits parricide into religion. According to Freud, Paul reached the conclusion that we are unhappy because we have killed God the Father. We were released from this sin only when Jesus Christ as Son sacrificed his life. The Son even takes the place of the Father: "Christianity, having arisen out of a father-religion, became a son-religion. It has not escaped the fate of having to get rid of the father."[15] Fear of the primordial father has been kept up in the most varied forms in Christianity.

A present-day reader (in this respect like most of the readers at the time, except of course in psychoanalytical circles) may regard this interpretation of the origin of religion as highly fictional, as a fantasy product unworthy of a scholar. He should remember two points. Firstly, Freud was writing at a time of great enthusiasm for the new evolutionary explanation of the world and religion, when the joy of discovery led to the construction of bold outlines of grades, of phases, and even of the detailed course of the evolution of religion. Things became different later, of course.

Secondly, looking back over the theories he had worked out Freud himself spoke very clearly of "hypotheses," "visions," "assumptions," "essays." But, despite their historical disputability and the universal criticism even of ethnologists and experts in the study of religions, he continued to uphold these views. Why?

Freud really had only a secondary interest in the historical question. For him, as we saw, it was really a question of a theory of religion established a priori which he then attempted to prove with the aid of material from the history of religion.

15. S. Freud, *Der Mann Moses und die monotheistische Religion* in *Studienausgabe* 9:580. (*Moses and Monotheism. Three Essays, S.E.* 23 [1964]: 3–137; quotation, p. 136.)

Even before seriously investigating the sources of primitive religion, in his article on Leonardo da Vinci (1910), he had anticipated the result of a psychoanalytical interpretation of religion: "Psycho-analysis has made us familiar with the intimate connection between the father-complex and belief in God; it has shown us that a personal God is, psychologically, nothing other than an exalted father, and it brings us evidence everyday of how young people lose their religious beliefs as soon as their father's authority breaks down. Thus we recognize that the roots of the need for religion are in the parental complex."[16]

The roots of the need for religion: from the psychological standpoint, the question of the origin of religion is closely linked with that of its essence.

What Is the Essence of Religion?

Four years before his death—in a postscript to his autobiography—Freud remarked that a "significant difference" was to be observed in his writings over the previous ten years, making much of what he had done in the past seem like a "detour": "My interest, after making a lifelong *detour* through the natural sciences, medicine and psychotherapy, returned to the cultural problems which had fascinated me long before, when I was a youth scarcely old enough for thinking."[17]

Religion takes first place among these problems of youth and

16. S. Freud, "Eine Kindheitserinnerung des Leonardo da Vinci" in *Studienausgabe* 10:146. Cf. the same author, *Totem und Tabu* in *Studienausgabe* 9:430 f. ("Leonardo da Vinci and a Memory of His Childhood" in *S.E.* 11 [1957]:123. Cf. *Totem and Taboo* in *S.E.* 13 [1957]:141 f.)

17. S. Freud, "Nachschrift," 1935 (to "Selbstdarstellung") in *Gesammelte Werke* 16:32. ("Postscript" to "An Autobiographical Study" in *S.E.* 20:72.)

age. Freud's main critical work on religion, *The Future of an Illusion* (1927) was the first of a series of studies which became his main preoccupation for the rest of his life, among these being *Civilisation and Its Discontents* (1930)[18] and finally his last great work, *Moses and Monotheism* (1939).[19] He deals with religion also at the end of the *New Introductory Lectures on Psycho-Analysis* (1933).[20]

What is religion? Freud now looks beyond religious rites and asks, what are "religious ideas"? He gives an exhaustive account of these in his *The Future of an Illusion*. What is new is that religion is no longer analyzed merely as historical, but mainly as a contemporary social phenomenon. "Religious ideas are teachings and assertions about facts and conditions of external (or internal) reality which tell something one has not discovered for oneself and which lay claim to one's belief."[21] But what is the basis of this claim? According to Freud three answers are given to this question, answers which are mutually contradictory and as a whole inadequate.

The first answer is that we should believe without demanding proofs. Freud asks why and suggests that it is because we are really aware of the fact that the claim is uncertain and without foundation.

The second answer is that we should believe because our forefathers believed. Freud points out that our ancestors were

18. S. Freud, *Das Unbehagen in der Kultur* (1930) in *Studienausgabe* 9:191–270. (*Civilisation and Its Discontents* in *S.E.*, 21 [1961]:59–145.)

19. S. Freud, *Der Mann Moses und die monotheistische Religion* (1939) in *Studienausgabe* 9:455–581. (*Moses and Monotheism* in *S.E.* 23 [1964]:3–137.)

20. S. Freud, *Neue Folge der Vorlesungen zur Einführung in die Psychoanalyse* (1933) in *Studienausgabe* 1:447–608, especially lecture 35, "Über eine Weltanschauung." (*New Introductory Lectures on Psycho-Analysis* in *S.E.* 22 [1964]: 1–182, especially lecture 35, "The Question of a Weltanschauung.")

21. S. Freud, *Die Zukunft einer Illusion* in *Studienausgabe* 9:159. (*The Future of an Illusion* in *S.E.* 21 [1961]:25.)

far more ignorant than we are and believed a great deal that we could not possibly believe today.

The third answer is that we should believe because we possess proofs handed down to us from primeval times. Freud asserts that the writings from which these proofs are drawn are untrustworthy, full of contradictions, frequently revised, and often downright false, and to invoke revelation is itself a proof that their doctrine is not authenticated. And if it is claimed that there are proofs belonging to the present time— those of the spiritualists, for instance—is it not clear that the great spirits they invoke, together with their trivial and silly answers, are so like themselves that it is easy to see the information for what it really is, the product of people who themselves provide no evidence of a spiritual reality independent of the body, of an immortal soul?

The "singular conclusion" to be drawn is that the most important statements, which are supposed to solve the riddles of the world for us and to reconcile us to all our suffering, are "the least well authenticated of any."[22] They are and were always obviously undemonstrable.

And yet we may wonder if it can be true that there is no reality at all behind religion. Despite defective authentication, have not religious ideas exercised the strongest influence of all on human beings? Where did they acquire their force? This too is a question that must be approached psychologically: the psychological origin of religion explains its essence. Freud now applies to the phenomenon of religion the model of wish-fulfillment discovered in dreams and neurotic symptoms. After gaining a deeper understanding of the structure of the unconscious, of instincts and of dreams, we can now understand

22. Ibid. 9:161. (S.E. 21:27.)

much better what we first heard from him about this subject, and it must now be stressed: religious ideas are "not precipitates of experiences or end-results of our thinking," but "*illusions, fulfilments of the oldest, strongest and most urgent wishes of mankind.* The secret of their strength lies in the strength of those wishes."[23] What wishes? The wishes of the childishly helpless human being for protection from life's perils, for the realization of justice in this unjust society, for the prolongation of earthly existence in a future life, for knowledge of the origin of the world, of the relationship between the corporeal and the mental. It is a question of projections (the dependence on Feuerbach is obvious). "The unclear, inner perception of one's own psychical apparatus stimulates thought-illusions which are naturally projected outwards and—characteristically—into the future and into a hereafter. Immortality, retribution, the whole hereafter, are such representations of our psychical interior . . . psychomythology."[24]

Yet all these wishes are infantile, rooted in "conflicts of childhood arising from the father-complex" and "never wholly overcome."[25] These are childhood conflicts in two senses, conflicts of the human individual and of the human race. The conflicts emerge, therefore, from the very earliest days of mankind, for the childhood of the individual is in fact a reproduction of the childhood of mankind, the ontogenesis of the human individual a reproduction of the phylogenesis of the human race. In both cases longing for a father is the root of religious needs; in both cases the Oedipus complex plays the main part. In *The Future of an Illusion*, therefore, Freud did not

23. Ibid. 9:164. (*S.E.* 21:30.)

24. Quoted from E. Wiesenhütter, "Verdrängter Glaube—Freuds Ende einer Illusion" in H. Zahrnt (ed.), *Jesus und Freud*, Munich, 1972, p. 68.

25. S. Freud, *Die Zukunft einer Illusion* in *Studienausgabe* 9:164. (*The Future of an Illusion* in *S.E.* 21 [1961]:30.)

revoke the historical-ethnological explanation of totemism and religion given in *Totem and Taboo*. In fact he confirmed it, placing the emphasis on the childish *helplessness* of the individual person and of mankind as a whole in face of the immense dangers threatening us from outside and from within ourselves. What has this helplessness to do with religion?

It is culture which creates and produces religious ideas in the individual. Like all other cultural attainments, religion springs from the necessity of defending oneself against the superpowers of nature and fate. How does this come about? Because impotent man in his perplexity and helplessness tries to unite himself to these superpowers and to influence them— in a word, naively and childishly to humanize and personify them. But, since he cannot associate with these menacing superpowers as with his equals, they acquire paternal characteristics. The need of protection and the longing for a father thus turn out to be identical. This means that impotent man creates gods for himself, both to be feared and to be won over, ambivalent nature-gods of fear and comfort.

Yet even when man gradually comes to appreciate the regularity and laws of natural phenomena, these gods do not lose their function. For "man's helplessness remains and along with it his longing for his father and the gods."[26] They retain their triple function: to banish the terrors of nature, to reconcile men to fate and death, and—since any culture is based on the necessity of work and the inhibition of instincts—to compensate men for all the suffering and privation of a common cultural life. With increasing knowledge of nature's laws, however, people concentrate their religious ideas on this third, moral function. The gods are supposed to offer men a higher

26. Ibid. 9:151 f. (*S.E.*, 21:17 f.)

purpose in life, an intelligence or providence superior to the world, a divine sanction for the moral precepts, a life after death. In this way the wisdom, infinite goodness and justice, and finally—with the Jews—the uniqueness of the divine being are made clear to men. Only at this stage, in regard to the one God, can a true child-father relationship emerge. For those people who are incapable of interiorizing the moral rules governing interpersonal relationships, the threat of divine punishments provides an additional motivation. But for the others such a threat of punishment is no longer necessary; on the contrary, if it is extended beyond the original, elementary precepts (prohibition of murder and incest) to all possible small, individual precepts, it is even harmful.

Religion, then, arose out of the oldest, strongest, and most urgent wishes of mankind. Religion is wishful thinking, illusion. "Illusion" means that religion is not a deliberate lie in the moral sense nor—and Freud stresses this—error in the epistemological sense; nor is it necessarily illusory in the sense of being unrealistic or opposed to reality. Illusion—and this is typical—is motivated by wish-fulfillment; it is a product of sensual-instinctual life and needs for its deciphering the decoding technique of applied psychology.

For Freud religious teachings as a whole are illusions, undemonstrable, and therefore no one can be compelled to believe them. It is true that they are at the same time irrefutable. And for that very reason they are certainly not credible. Some of them, indeed, are so improbable from the psychological standpoint that they amount to delusions (here Freud's old idea of rites as obsessive actions is extended to religious doctrines). But religious doctrines differ from illusions insofar as they are not—as we saw—necessarily false. For it could be that . . .

It should be noted that Freud is concerned only with the

psychological nature of religious ideas (as illusions), not with their truth content (as reality). "To assess the truth-value of religious doctrine does not lie within the scope of the present enquiry. It is enough for us that we have recognized them as being, in their psychological nature, illusions."[27] Of course Freud does not conceal the fact that the psychological derivation of religion has powerfully influenced his attitude to its truth content, especially since we know today more or less at what times and for what motives particular religious doctrines arose. "We shall tell ourselves that it would be very nice if there were a moral order in the universe and an after-life; but it is a very striking fact that all this is exactly as we are bound to wish it to be. And it would be more remarkable still if our wretched, ignorant and downtrodden ancestors had succeeded in solving all these difficult riddles of the universe."[28]

Education for Reality

Would it not be sad, however, if religion, which has done so much for culture, were to disappear? Could man sustain at all the great hardships of life without the consolation of religion? Freud coolly answers that religion has had time in the course of millennia to show what it could do for men's happiness. Obviously it did not do enough, for the majority of people are still unhappy in this civilization of ours. But was not religion the support of morality? That is true, but it was at the same time the support of immorality. In order to preserve the submissiveness of the masses toward religion, great concessions were made to man's instinctual nature.

In our time, however, the influence of religion is increasingly

27. Ibid. 9:167. (*S.E.* 21:33.)
28. Ibid. 9:167. (*S.E.* 21:33.)

on the decline. The reason for this is "the increase of the scientific spirit in the higher strata of human society." "Criticism has whittled away the evidential value of religious documents, natural science has shown up the errors in them, and comparative research has been struck by the fatal resemblance between the religious ideas which we revere and the mental products of primitive peoples and times. . . . In this process there is no stopping."[29] According to Freud, religion as the universal human obsessional neurosis ultimately stemming from the Oedipus complex is inexorably disappearing.

If, however, we want to forestall the dangers of such a process of dissolution, especially for the morality of the uneducated and oppressed masses, a thorough revision of the relations between religion and culture is needed, a new, rationally substantiated Weltanschauung which leaves out God and admits the purely human origin of all cultural institutions and regulations. This means a purely rational justification of the prohibition of murder and of all cultural regulations, not in virtue of divine revelation but on the basis of social necessity. However overwhelming our feelings, our instinctual wishes, they must be controlled: by intelligence, by reason, which must no longer be stultified by early training, by religious prohibitions on thinking and the inhibition of thought about sex. Consequently an attempt should be made at irreligious education. One thing we must not do and that is to abolish religion by force and at one stroke.

"Education for reality." Both for the individual human being and for mankind as a whole religion is a pubertal, transitional phase of human development. Neither as individual nor as species can man remain a child forever. He must grow up, he must master reality with his own resources and with the aid of

29. Ibid. 9:172. (S.E. 21:38.)

science and at the same time learn to resign himself to the inescapable necessities of fate. To leave heaven to the angels and the sparrows (Freud quotes the poem *Deutschland, ein Wintermärchen*, by his fellow unbeliever, Heinrich Heine), abandon expectations of a hereafter and concentrate all the resources thus liberated on earthly life, this is the task of the mature, adult human being. "Of what use to him is the mirage of wide acres on the moon, whose harvest no one has ever yet seen?"[30]

Admittedly, even this rational procedure may leave scope for illusions. But these illusions can be corrected and they are not delusions, like those of religion. In the long run it is impossible to resist reason and experience and the opposition of religion to both is striking. No, the voice of reason can still secure a hearing despite all unreason. Our God—Logos—gradually actualizes the wishes permitted by nature. Faith in science, in knowledge acquired by verifiable experience, provides a support which is lacking to the believer in God. "We believe that it is possible for scientific work to gain some knowledge about the reality of the world, by means of which we can increase our power and in accordance with which we can arrange our life. If this belief is an illusion, then we are in the same position as you. But science has given us evidence by its numerous and important successes that it is no illusion."[31] At the end of the book, Freud repeats this with rare pathos: "No, our science is no illusion. But an illusion it would be to suppose that what science cannot give us we can get elsewhere."[32]

Half a century later, in the last chapter of the *New Introduc-*

30. Ibid. 9:183. (*S.E.* 21:50.)
31. Ibid. 9:188. (*S.E.* 21:55.)
32. Ibid. 9:189. Cf. also the comments in *Das Unbehagen in der Kultur* in *Studienausgabe* 9:206. (*S.E.* 21:56; cf. also *Civilisation and Its Discontents* in *S.E.* 21:70.)

tory Lectures on Psycho-Analysis (1933), "The Question of a *Weltanschauung*," Freud returns to the relationship between religion and science. Is psychoanalysis itself a Weltanschauung? Freud's answer is quite clearly negative and he sums it up at the end: "Psycho-analysis, in my opinion, is incapable of creating a *Weltanschauung* of its own. It does not need one; it is a part of science and can adhere to the scientific *Weltanschauung*."[33]

But it is precisely religion which is the greatest opponent of this scientific Weltanschauung: "Of the three powers which may dispute the basic position of science, religion alone is to be taken seriously as an enemy."[34] Not art, not philosophy, but religion is the "immense power which has the strongest emotions of human beings at its service" and "it constructed a *Weltanschauung*, consistent and self-contained to an unparalleled degree, which, although it has been profoundly shaken, persists to this day."[35] Never did Freud speak more clearly of the "grandiose nature of religion" and of "what it undertakes to do for human beings" by simultaneously exercising three functions: "It gives information about the origin and coming into existence of this universe, it assures them of its protection and of ultimate happiness in the ups and downs of life and it directs their thoughts and actions by precepts which it lays down with its whole authority."[36] At one and the same time, therefore, it provides instruction and consolation and imposes demands.

But never did Freud submit religion to such close criticism as he did here by gathering together and expanding with concen-

---

33. S. Freud, *Neue Folge der Vorlesungen zur Einführung in die Psychoanalyse* in *Studienausgabe* 1:608. (*New Introductory Lectures on Psycho-Analysis* in *S.E.* 22 [1964]:181.)
34. Ibid. 1:588. (*S.E.* 22:160.)
35. Ibid. 1:588 f. (*S.E.* 22:161.)
36. Ibid. 1:589. (*S.E.* 22:161.)

trated force, systematically and consistently, what he had written twenty years before in his book on totemism and six years before in his treatment of religion as illusion:

> In summary, therefore, the judgement of science on the religious *Weltanschauung* is this. While the different religions wrangle with one another as to which of them is in possession of the truth, our view is that the question of the truth of religious beliefs may be left altogether on one side. Religion is an attempt to master the sensory world in which we are situated by means of the wishful world which we have developed within us as a result of biological and psychological necessities. But religion cannot achieve this. Its doctrines bear the imprint of the times in which they arose, the ignorant times of the childhood of humanity. Its consolations deserve no trust. Experience teaches us that the world is no nursery. The ethical demands on which religion seeks to lay stress need, rather, to be given another basis; for they are indispensable to human society and it is dangerous to link obedience to them with religious faith. If we attempt to assign the place of religion in the evolution of mankind, it appears not as a permanent acquisition but as a counterpart to the neurosis which individual civilised men have to go through in their passage from childhood to maturity.[37]

Against any kind of religion, Freud declares himself in favor of a "scientific Weltanschauung." Admittedly, with an appropriate dose of skepticism, for—after a brief discussion of nihilism and Marxism as well—the *New Introductory Lectures* conclude: "A *Weltanschauung* erected upon science has, apart from its emphasis on the real external world, mainly negative traits, such as submission to the truth and rejection of illu-

37. Ibid. 1:595. (*S.E.* 22:168.)

sions. Any of our fellow-men who is dissatisfied with this state
of things, who calls for more than this for his momentary
consolation, may look for it where he can find it. We shall not
grudge it him, we cannot help him, but nor can we on his
account think differently."[38]

After this destructive criticism, however, is it not surprising
that Freud, from his eightieth year, continued to study religion
intensively and devoted to it almost the greater part of the
remaining five years of his life? Is it surprising that he reflected
again on the origins of the Jewish and Christian religions, in
order now to bring out, not only the psychological, but also the
historical truth, particularly of monotheistic religion, to show
how this also rests on the unconscious memory of actual
events? At the same time—and incidentally with considerable
hesitation—he committed himself to a very bold reconstruction of the Moses legend. According to this, Moses was an
Egyptian who had accepted the monotheistic faith of the
pharaoh Akhenaton and converted the Jews to it; he was killed
in a rebellion, leaving the Jewish people with a lasting unconscious sense of guilt. The murder of the prophet in monotheistic religion corresponds to the murder of the primordial father
in totemism and the murder of the Son of God in Christianity:
all consequences of the Oedipus complex.

Originally entitled *The Man Moses. An Historical Novel*, this
work was published in three separate papers. Part of the third
was read by his daughter Anna at the Paris International
Psycho-Analytical Congress in 1938. In 1939 the work appeared in German with the title *Der Mann Moses und die
monotheistische Religion (The Man Moses and Monotheistic
Religion)*. It was the year World War II began and also the year
Freud died.

38. Ibid. 1:608. (*S.E.* 22:182.)

CRITIQUE OF FREUD

3

Freud himself in his main critical work on religion raised the question "whether the publication of this work might not, after all, do harm. Not to a person, however, but to a cause—the cause of psycho-analysis."[1] In fact for a long time, and not least under the influence of the churches, psychoanalysis has been identified in public opinion with irreligiousness and sexuality, with the breakdown of religion, order, and morality.

But despite all the "noise" of opponents—which was to be expected—and all the difficulties created for his fellow workers, "some of whom do not by any means share my attitude to the problems of religion," Freud maintained his standpoint. "In point of fact psycho-analysis is a method of research, an impartial instrument, like the infinitesimal calculus, as it were. . . . If the application of the psycho-analytic method makes it possible to find a new argument against the truths of religion, *tant pis* for religion; but defenders of religion will by the same right make use of psycho-analysis in order to give full value to the affective significance of religious doctrines."[2] This is what in fact happened. And it was not least the differing approaches to sexuality and religion which led Freud and his friends—particularly Freud, Adler, and Jung—to part from and later to oppose one another.

The Horizon of Psychoanalytic Criticism

Depth psychology (like *schizophrenia* and *ambivalence*) is an expression we owe to the famous Zurich psychiatrist Eugen Bleuler, who was Jung's teacher. What was and remained common to Freud, Adler, and Jung—the famous "triple-star of

1. S. Freud, *Die Zukunft einer Illusion* in *Studienausgabe* 9:170 (*The Future of an Illusion* in *S.E.* 21 [1961]:36.)
2. Ibid. 9:170. (*S.E.* 21:36–37.)

depth psychology"—in contrast to all former psychologists, was their theoretical and practical concern with the depths of the human psyche, with the underground of human behavior, that is, with the unconscious. This was to be understood scientifically, methodically rendered accessible, and opened up therapeutically, particularly by means of dream analysis, but increasingly also by other therapeutical methods and especially with the aid of various tests. It thus became possible to obtain a deeper insight into human reality, with scarcely foreseeable consequences for the individual and for society, not only for medicine, psychiatry, and psychology, but also for educational theory, the human sciences, the science of religion, and human behavior as a whole.

Freud's theory, however, had raised very serious questions, particularly for his friends who had gone their own way. Is it right to understand the unconscious so very negatively, as a reservoir of repressed wishes? Is it right to consider instinct mechanistically, merely from the standpoint of causality? Is it right to ascribe all intentions beyond the instinct for self-preservation to sexual wishes, to the libido, even if with Freud we understand *sexual* in a broader sense? Is it right to understand the individual structure of the psyche merely retrospectively, in the light of past events, instead of prospectively, in the light of a meaning and purpose in life which a person has decided upon for himself or adopted from elsewhere?

In 1911 Alfred Adler (1870—1937), a practicing doctor, gave four lectures under the heading of "A Critique of the Freudian Sexual Theory of Mental Life."[3] Like Freud, Adler was of Jewish descent, but a convinced socialist and later a friend of

3. A. Adler, "Zur Kritik der Freudschen Sexualtheorie des Seelenlebens" (1911) in A. Adler and C. Fortmüller, *Heilen und Bilden. Ein Buch der Erziehungskunst für Ärzte und Pädagogen.* New edition prepared by W. Metzger, Frankfurt, 1973, pp. 94–113.

Trotsky; for a decade or so he had been a member of Freud's circle of friends and was now president of the Vienna group of the Psycho-Analytical Union. The lectures led to his being "excommunicated," together with seven other doctors, from the group around Sigmund Freud. A year later, in his work *The Neurotic Constitution*,[4] he laid the foundations of the Individual Psychology with which his name was to be associated in the future. The object of its teaching and the goal of its psychotherapeutic practice (and later particularly of its educational theory) was the integral, free, purposeful "in-dividual," responsible for his actions. Unlike Freud's analyzing, dissecting method, Adler's approach is directed more to the human being in his wholeness and to his projected life plan in this world.

For Adler the starting point of his scientific theory and the explanatory principle of mental disorders is not the conflict between the ego and the sexual instinct, but the striving for superiority, which is likewise found already in the child as it builds and destroys and struggles for recognition by the adults, the "striving for power," as Adler's most outstanding student, Fritz Künkel, put it. From the investigation of "organ inferiority"[5] Adler came to discover the "inferiority feeling."[6] Neuroses accordingly are not to be interpreted causally, as the consequences of infantile and unconsciously operative traumas, but purposively, as the expressions of an "inferiority feeling" which is continually nourished by new, negative experiences of life

4. A. Adler, *Über den Nervösen Charakter. Grundzüge einer vergleichenden Individual-Psychologie und Psychotherapie*, Wiesbaden, 1912; 4th edition, 1928; reprinted Frankfurt, 1972. (English translation, *The Neurotic Constitution. Outline of a Comparative Individualistic Psychology and Psychotherapy*, Kegan Paul, London, 1917/Moffat-Yard, New York, 1917.)

5. A. Adler, *Studie über Minderwertigkeit von Organen*, Vienna, 1907. (English translation, *Study of Organ Inferiority and Its Psychical Compensation: a Contribution to Clinical Medicine*, New York, 1917.)

6. Cf. A. Adler, *Über den nervösen Charakter*, Frankfurt, 1912, pp. 38–57. (English translation, *The Neurotic Constitution*, London and New York, 1917.)

preventing the person from reaching his goals and for which he is "compensated"—often "over-compensated"—by the "instinct to dominate." As opposed to the innumerable false adjustments, the common feature of which is the "ego-centering" ("ego-attachment") of human experience and behavior as a whole, Adler insists that the authentic normal state is the centering on the group in "community feeling" ("social interest") and on the given task at any particular time (the requirement of "striving for perfection" or—according to Künkel—of "objectivity"). There can be no happiness for the individual at the expense of others, but—without wanting to hunt it down or extort it—only together with others. The "inferiority feeling" must be overcome by "community feeling." This then is the objective of a "comparative individual and community psychology."[7]

Carl Gustav Jung (1875–1961), even before his collaboration with Freud (from 1907), was well known as a psychiatrist because of his experimental studies of affectively toned complexes.[8] Twelve months after Adler's departure, he too sepa-

---

7. Cf. also A. Adler, *Menschenkenntnis*, 1927, reprinted Frankfurt, 1966; and the same author, "Vorträge zur Einführung in die Psychotherapie für Ärzte, Psychologen und Lehrer" published under the title *Praxis und Theorie der Individualpsychologie*, 1930, new impression, Darmstadt, 1965. (English translations: *Understanding Human Nature*, Greenberg, New York/Allen & Unwin, London, 1928, new impression, 1968; *The Practice and Theory of Individual Psychology*, Harcourt Brace, New York, 1924/Routledge and Kegan Paul, London, 1923, 2d revised edition, 1929, new impression, 1964.)

8. Cf. C. G. Jung, "Über die Psychologie der Dementia praecox. Ein Versuch," 1907, now with the same title in "Frühe Schriften II," in *Studienausgabe*, Olten, 1972. Cf. in the same edition "Frühe Schriften I" ("Psychiatrie und Okkultismus," especially Jung's dissertation on occult phenomena), and "Frühe Schriften III" ("Zur Psychoanalyse"). (English translations, "The Psychology of Dementia Praecox," pp. 1–151 in *The Psychogenesis of Mental Disease*, vol. 3 of *Collected Works*, Routledge and Kegan Paul, London/Pantheon, New York, 1960; "On the Psychology and Pathology of So-Called Occult Phenomena," pp. 3–88 in *Psychiatric Studies*, vol. I of *Collected Works*, London and New York, 1957; "Concerning Psychoanalysis," pp. 78–81 in *Freud and Psychoanalysis*, vol. 4 of *Collected Works*, London and New York, 1961.)

rated from Freud, because—as he showed in his early work *Symbols of Transformation* (1912)[9]—he rejected the latter's sexual theory and conception of the libido. In 1914 Jung retired as president of the International Psycho-Analytical Society and later cut himself off completely from it. Subsequently he attempted to overcome Freud's and Adler's lack of balance by a greater differentiation and a more comprehensive grasp of the problems and to analyze the human psyche—this totality of all psychic processes, both conscious and unconscious—in the whole complexity of its relationships and potentialities. Hence, in contrast to Freud's "psychoanalysis" and Adler's "Individual Psychology," he called his theory "Analytical Psychology" or "Complex Psychology."

According to Jung, libido must not be understood exclusively as man's sexual drive. It must be understood as undifferentiated psychic energy which is governed especially by the laws of conservation of energy and of entropy, by causality, but also by finality, and which lies behind the four different mental processes (thinking, feeling, sensation, intuition). Consequently four basic types of psychic functions are to be distinguished: the rational, evaluating functions of thinking (distinguishing true from false) and feeling (distinguishing pleasant from unpleasant); the irrational, purely perceptive functions of sensation (concerned with external data) and intuition (concerned with the internal, the enigmatic, the essential). At the same time two modes of approach or reaction must be noted: a person is either extraverted (influenced mainly by objective factors) or introverted (influenced mainly by subjective factors). On the basis of these different modes of functioning and

9. C. G. Jung, *Wandlungen und Symbole der Libido*, Vienna, 1912; 4th revised edition under the title *Symbole der Wandlung* (1952) in *Gesammelte Werke*, vol. 5, Zurich and Stuttgart, 1973. (English translation, *Symbols of Transformation* in *Collected Works*, vol. 5, London and New York, 1956.)

reacting Jung establishes his eight psychological types.[10] The extraverted type is either predominantly a thinking type, a feeling type, a sensation type, or an intuitive type; so too with the introverted type. This predominant function can be described as the superior function in relation to its opposite, inferior function (thinking and feeling are opposites, as are sensation and intuition). The inferior function will be powerful in the unconscious, especially in the second half of life, and will seek a compensatory balance. In any single individual the other two functions are called auxiliary functions.

According to Jung the dark side of the soul, its "shadow," should be made conscious, "accepted" and brought into the realm of personal responsibility; the element of the opposite sex in a person (for a man the *anima*, for a woman the *animus*), also should be differentiated and realized in us; the *persona*, the face which we show (as protection or mask) to others, should be brought into the right relationship to our ego. Only in this way, in the process of coming to be himself (individuation), does a person develop his individual self, which is responsible for the integration and stability of the personality, the unity of the person in an authentic combination of consciousness and the unconscious. Neuroses are disturbances of this individuation process.

Adler's and Jung's corrections and further developments—which are important for the understanding of religion—must be noted here. At the same time it cannot be our task to judge among Freud, Adler, and Jung or among their schools, nor to examine the repercussions of the work of Adler and Jung on Freud. Otherwise it would be necessary to explain a number of things: how Freud from the very beginning distinguished be-

10. C. G. Jung, *Psychologische Typen* (1920), 9th revised edition in *Gesammelte Werke*, vol. 6, Zurich and Stuttgart, 1960. (English translation, *Psychological Types*, vol. 6 of *Collected Works*, Routledge and Kegan Paul, London/Princeton University Press, Princeton, 1971.)

tween the sexual instinct and the instinct for self-preservation (later, ego), but examined only the sexual instinct at length; then later (tacitly admitting that Adler was right) turned his attention to the aggressive character of these instincts; how finally, after further modification of his theory of instinct, he conceded a fundamental and autonomous status to the phenomena of aggression and obstructiveness by distinguishing between two types of instinct: life-instinct (libido) and death-instinct (destruction, aggression), the great powers Eros and Thanatos.[11]

In particular it cannot be our task to discuss the great specific themes of Adler's Individual Psychology: for instance, the mother's over-solicitude and her pampering of the child, the dethronement of the firstborn and the conflicts among brothers and sisters, the project of a life-plan already present in childhood and directed to a fictive goal, the revolt of woman in "manly protest," striving for recognition as an attempt to conquer the feeling of insecurity and inferiority. Nor can it be our task to get involved in the controversy about certain theories of Jung in the field of depth psychology: in addition to those mentioned above, the theories of the individual and collective unconscious, of archetypes, of symbols and myths. For our consideration all that is really important is the *complex of problems relating to religion,* and it is just at this point that both Adler and Jung differ essentially from Freud.

In his analysis of religion Adler does not start out from the father complex. In fact, with an explicit allusion to Freud's "drive psychology," he dissociates himself from this standpoint. He sees in this "mechanistic view" an "illusion," since "it is without goal and direction."[12]

11. Cf. R. Wollheim, *Sigmund Freud,* London, 1971, chap. 7.
12. A. Adler, "Religion und Individualpsychologie" in A. Adler and E. Jahn, *Religion und Individualpsychologie. Eine prinzipielle Auseinandersetzung über Menschenführung,* 1933, new impression Frankfurt, 1975, pp. 68–98, quota-

The point from which Adler really starts out in his definition of religion is the "constant inferiority feeling of distressed humanity." "God, eternally complete," says Adler, "is to date the most brilliant manifestation of the goal of perfection" of man. This means: "The idea of God and its immense significance for mankind can be understood and appreciated from the viewpoint of Individual Psychology as concretization and interpretation of the human recognition of greatness and perfection, and as commitment of the individual as well as of society to a goal which rests in man's future and which in the present heightens the driving force by enhancing the feelings and emotions."[13]

It thus becomes clear that, for Adler, religion and Individual Psychology meet in "the goal of perfection of mankind." He can be tolerant in regard to religion, as long as it serves this purpose: "I would acknowledge as valuable any movement which guarantees in its final goal the welfare of all."[14] This is the attitude of a man who regards his Individual Psychology as "the heir to all great movements whose aim is the welfare of mankind."[15] For, despite all his tolerance in regard to religion, it is quite clear to Adler that God is an idea, albeit the supreme and greatest idea of mankind, the idea of perfection for which man is longing. But for Adler too the ultimate reality is man. Man is the center of reality and it is the function of Individual Psychology "to make him the center."[16] Thus, although unat-

---

tion, p. 70. Cf. also A. Adler, *Der Sinn des Lebens*, 1933, new impression, Frankfurt, 1973, especially the last chapter. (English translation, "Religion and Individual Psychology" in A. Adler, *Superiority and Social Interest*, Routledge and Kegan Paul, London, 1965, pp. 271–308, quotation, p. 277. Cf. also A. Adler, *Social Interest*, Faber, London, 1949.)

13. A. Adler, *Religion und Individualpsychologie*, p. 69. (English translation, *Superiority and Social Interest*, p. 276.)

14. Ibid., p. 73. (English translation, p. 280.)

15. Ibid., p. 98. (English translation, pp. 307–08.)

16. Ibid., p. 70. (English translation, p. 277.)

tainable, the goal is set for mankind in a continually ascending, vast evolutionary process. "Whether one calls the highest effective goal deity, or socialism, or"—as Adler does—"the pure idea of social interest, . . . it always reflects the same ruling, perfection-promising, grace-giving goal of overcoming."[17]

Ernst Jahn, a student of Adler and a theologian, clearly perceived the problem that becomes apparent at this point and insisted on it in replying to Adler: "This is the question which is not fully clarified: Is God an idea, a goal, or reality? The Christian interpretation is that God is neither idea nor goal. He is reality. Ideas and goals can be determined by the power of human thinking. But God's being is not tied to human thought-processes. God is not the result of thinking. God is overwhelming reality."[18] Of course one may ask how Jahn can be so certain. For Adler, the psychologist, God "is a gift of faith."[19] Unlike Freud's psychoanalysis, faith does not lack "the goal which signifies life," but—since God is not scientifically demonstrable—what is lacking is the "causal foundation."[20] For Jahn, the theologian, it is the very opposite: "Faith is a gift of God."[21] But is this not really wishful thinking? Freud's radical question has not yet been answered.

Jung expressly dissociates himself from the atheism of Freud's work on religion as illusion. Younger than Freud by a generation, he says that the latter's standpoint "is based on the rationalistic materialism of the scientific views current in the late nineteenth century."[22] At the time that book was pub-

---

17. Ibid., p. 70. (English translation, pp. 277–78.)
18. E. Jahn in Adler and Jahn, *Religion und Individualpsychologie*, p. 99. (Jahn's epilogue is not included in the English translation.)
19. A. Adler, *Religion und Individualpsychologie*, p. 70. (English translation, p. 277.)
20. Ibid., p. 70. (English translation, p. 277.)
21. E. Jahn, in Adler and Jahn, *Religion und Individualpsychologie*, p. 100.
22. C. G. Jung, "Psychoanalyse und Seelsorge" (1928–29) in *Psychologie und*

lished, he turned clearly against "medical incursions into religion and philosophy, to which doctors naively believe themselves entitled (witness the explanation of religious processes in terms of sexual symbols or infantile wish-fantasies)."[23] While Freud uncompromisingly rejects religion as such and Adler benevolently tolerates it, Jung's attitude is in principle friendly toward it. But how far does this friendliness extend?

Jung alone of the three concentrates seriously on the psychological dimension of the contents of religious faith: the doctrine of God (the Trinity), Christology, Mariology, the sacraments and especially confession and the Mass, all these are examined in lengthy studies.[24] At the same time, however, his standpoint is exclusively psychological-phenomenological. In other words, he is asking not about historical but only about psychological truth. "When psychology speaks, for instance, of the motif of the virgin birth, it is only concerned with the fact that there is such an idea, but it is not concerned with the question whether such an idea is true or false in any other sense. The idea is psychologically true in as much as it exists. Psychological existence is subjective in so far as an idea occurs in only one individual. But it is objective in so far as that idea is shared by a society—by a *consensus gentium*."[25] But can psy-

Religion, *Studienausgabe*, Olten, 1971, pp. 155–61, quotation, p. 156. (English translation, "Psychoanalysis and the Cure of Souls" in *Psychology and Religion: West and East*, pp. 348–54 in vol. 11 of *Collected Works*, quotation, p. 349.)

23. Ibid., p. 160. (English translation, p. 353.)

24. Cf. especially C. G. Jung, "Das Wandlungssymbol in der Messe" (1940–41) in *Psychologie und Religion*, *Studienausgabe*, Olten, 1971, pp. 163–267. (English translation, "Transformation Symbolism in the Mass" in *Psychology and Religion: West and East*, pp. 201–96 of vol. 11 of *Collected Works*.)

25. C. G. Jung, "Psychologie und Religion" (1939) in *Psychologie und Religion*, *Studienausgabe*, Olten, 1971, pp. 11–127, quotation, p. 12. (English translation, "Psychology and Religion," pp. 3–105 of *Psychology and Religion: West and East*, vol. 11 of *Collected Works*, quotation, p. 6.)

chological truth (that is, psychological existence) be so clearly distinguished from actual, historical truth? Erich Fromm in his criticism of Jung's view of religion rightly observes: "Even the practising psychiatrist could not work were he not concerned with the truth of an idea. . . . Otherwise he could not speak of a delusion or a paranoid system."[26]

Later Jung became more clearly aware of the limits of his psychological method. Psychological research does not at all mean a "psychologizing, that is, an annihilation of the mystery." "To treat a metaphysical statement as a psychic process is not to say that it is 'merely psychic', as my critics assert—in the fond belief that the word 'psychic' postulates something known. It does not seem to have occurred to people that when we say "psyche" we are alluding to the densest darkness it is possible to imagine. The ethics of the researcher require him to admit where his knowledge comes to an end. This end is the beginning of wisdom."[27] But it is still not clear whether God is regarded as a part of the human psyche or as distinct from it.

Despite all his skepticism in regard to ecclesiastical and denominational Christianity, Jung himself always wanted to remain a Christian. In the last year of his life he wrote to a Belgian theologian: "To be exact, I must say that, although I profess myself a Christian, I am at the same time convinced that the chaotic contemporary situation shows that present-day Christianity is not the final truth. Further progress is an absolute necessity since the present state of affairs seems to me insupportable. As I see it, the contributions of the psychology of the unconscious should be taken into account."[28]

26. E. Fromm, *Psychoanalysis and Religion*, Yale University Press, New Haven, 1950, pp. 15–16.

27. C. G. Jung, *Psychologie und Religion, Studienausgabe*, p. 267. (English translation, p. 296.)

28. C. G. Jung, *Briefe*, edited by A. Jaffé with the collaboration of G. Adler, 3

Adler and Jung in their views of religion qualified Freud's
critique of religion in important points. But even Jung's more
friendly approach to religion still leaves unanswered Freud's
fundamental question: Despite its positive function is not religion, nevertheless, merely wishful thinking? However significant the idea of God may be in psychological terms, is not
God a "purely psychological" reality? Or—to adopt Jung's
terminology—if God is undoubtedly "psychologically existent,"
that is, a "psychological truth,"—subjectively in the human
individual, objectively in a larger group—does he also exist
independently of our consciousness, of our psyche? Before turning again to this question—which had been the subject of
debate earlier by Feuerbach and Marx—in its psychological
aspects, we must first examine Freud's answer to the question
of the origin of religion, which prepares the way for his answer
to the question of its essence.

The Disputed Origins of Religion

Nowhere did Freud find less support than for his views on
ethnology and history of religion. The reason ethnologists and
anthropologists did not deal adequately with his theses from
the very beginning may have been that they were all convinced
that there was no point in serious discussion, that Freud had
misunderstood the material. As always, the theories based on
the history of religion, which Freud used to substantiate what
we saw to be his preconceived view of the Oedipus complex as
the origin of religion, are scarcely defended in their pure form
by experts in the field of religious studies today. Neither the

---

vols., Olten and Fribourg, 1973, 3:322 f. (English translation, C. G. Jung,
Letters, selected and edited by Gerhard Adler, in collaboration with Aniela
Jaffé, 2 vols., Routledge and Kegan Paul, London/Princeton University Press,
Princeton, 1973–75, vol. 2, 1975, p. 575.)

animistic nor the preanimistic, neither the magical nor the totemistic theory of the origin of religion has succeeded in gaining acceptance.

What was questioned was not primarily the abundant factual material which had been collected by such reputable researchers as Tylor and Marett, Frazer and Robertson Smith. It was the interpretation of the collected material that came under criticism, for example, the conception of *mana* as an impersonal fluid power outside the control of individuals, animatism attributing life to all things, or the combination of totemism and exogamy. Above all, the incorporation of the very heterogeneous material into a preconceived evolutionary scheme was called into question.

Obviously no serious scholar today disputes the evidence of evolution in the history of religion. Even religions have gone through a process of development. To that extent Freud, with the ethnologists, has proved to be right, as opposed to all theologians thinking in terms of a static and immobile reality. Nevertheless, all serious scholars today question the imposition of a doctrinaire systematic evolutionism on the history of religion. Religions have developed in a wholly and entirely unsystematic pluriformity. It is admitted, however, that, in the postulated primitive phases of religion, magic and belief in souls or spirits certainly played a prominent role in many religions; certainly some deified ancestors have been worshipped as divine beings; certainly in many cases the worship of a totem animal has passed over into worship of gods. But the claim that preanimism or animism or totemism was everywhere the original form of religion is a dogmatic postulate, not a historically proved fact.

What have simply not been proved historically are precisely the assumptions of the evolutionary scheme: that religion ever developed uniformly; that a particular religion passed through the different phases; that religion universally developed out of magic, ideas of holiness from taboo, belief in spirits from belief in souls, belief in gods from belief in spirits, belief in God from belief in gods. Even what is presumed to be the most primitive stage—belief in souls or spirits—is not found among all nature-peoples and particularly not in the supposedly oldest cultures. In the light of ethnology, history of religion, and development psychology, animistic ideas are not original, but later, derived phenomena. From this very fact it becomes clear why the alleged sequence of the different phases could not hitherto be proved in the case of any single religion. The individual phenomena and phases interpenetrate. Instead of talking about phases or epochs it seems more appropriate now to speak of strata or structures which in principle can be found in all phases or epochs.

Today we have become distrustful of neatly worked out structures and we are inclined to question their problematic *assumptions*. Is it so certain that the European or American type of intellectual with all his enlightenment is really superior to the people—especially the "primitives"—whose lives are governed by these religions but whose knowledge is so much more vital and existential? Is it so certain that there is no reality at all behind the religious belief and action of these "primitives" and that their whole attitude arises from a mistake (which needs to be clarified)? Are religions then from the very outset less true than science? Or has science perhaps reached the limits of its resources at the point where it seeks to probe a living religion and the wholly different knowledge of "primitive" human beings with the aid of "geometrical," rational knowledge? Is there any justification at all for seeking in principle to explain religious factors in the light of nonreligious, to explain religion in the light of magic? Is this the way to advance toward an understanding of what is genuinely religious? And does the relationship between lower and higher cultures coincide with the relationship between lower and higher religions? Is it possible at all to distinguish so sharply and unequivocally between primitive and higher religions?

In the very year of the publication of *Totem and Taboo*, Émile Durkheim,[29] one of the founders of modern sociology—with an eye particularly to certain primitive Australian peoples—objected to the picture prevalent at the time of primitive religion as an empty, abstruse tissue of superstition. Even these primitive religions had a core of reality, which, however, Durkheim found not in a divine power but in society, in the clan, the symbol or emblem of which is the totem.

The evolutionary scheme was, however, first directly attacked by the Scots writer Andrew Lang.[30] The anthropologist Wilhelm Schmidt followed him with an enormous twelve-volume work on the origin of religion.[31] Using the method of Frobenius and others he attempted, along with his students, to demonstrate the thesis that the oldest religion was not animism, preanimism, or totemism, but "primitive monotheism." Here an anti-evolutionary scheme was set up against the evolutionary scheme. It certainly seems possible to show that there were primitive tribes who believed, not in spirits, but in a "High God" (primordial or universal Father as father of the tribe or of heaven), although the latter, oddly enough, has little or no place in worship and apparently, as "originator," merely represents an answer to the question of the source of things. These high gods might be something

29. E. Durkheim, *Les formes élémentaires de la vie religieuse. Le système totémique en Australie*, Paris, 1912, 5th edition, 1968.
30. Andrew Lang, *The Making of Religion*, London, 1898; the same author, *Magic and Religion*, London, 1901.
31. Wilhelm Schmidt, *Der Ursprung der Gottesidee*, 12 vols., Münster, 1912–55. (English translation, [abridged], *The Origin and Growth of Religion*, London, 1931.)

primary and not merely derived from lower grades. But their antiquity and their nature are disputed by scholars. There is a lack of clarity especially on the questions whether these "primitive peoples" are really primitive in a historical sense, whether such a supreme God excludes other gods (monotheism) or includes them ("henotheism"), whether his nature is to be understood as active or as passive (in the latter event he would be otiose).

But however much the studies of Lang, Schmidt, and lastly of the German ethnologist A. E. Jensen[32] have shaken the evolutionary scheme, they have *not proved the central thesis* which they wanted to prove, namely, that the primordial religion is precisely this High God religion and not animism. The theological interest behind the anti-evolutionary scheme was obvious. This thesis of primitive monotheism was intended to demonstrate historically the fact of a "primitive revelation," a consideration which has in fact been an obstacle to scholarly discussion.

It has, then, become increasingly clear that *neither* the theory of degeneration from a lofty monotheistic beginning *nor* the evolutionary theory of a lower animistic or preanimistic beginning can be historically substantiated in a definite manner. Both are essentially dogmatic systems, the first in the guise of a theologically inspired natural science and the other in the guise of rationalistic natural science. Not only has the primordial religion not hitherto been found. Scientifically it simply *cannot be found*. Hence—and a consensus is already emerging on this point—the search should be called off. People have come to realize, and this of course must also go for Freud's

32. Adolf E. Jensen, *Mythos und Kult bei Naturvölkern*, Wiesbaden, 1951. (English translation, *Myth and Cult among Primitive Peoples*, University of Chicago Press, London and Chicago, 1963.)

theory, that the sources necessary for a historical explanation
of the origin of religion are simply not available. Contemporary
nature-peoples are not historically "primitive peoples": like
civilized people, they have a long, albeit unwritten history
behind them. As Freud himself actually indicated, without
however drawing strict conclusions from it, as far as the origin
of religion is concerned, we cannot get beyond historical and
psychological "hypotheses," "visions," "presumptions," "essays."

On the other hand, today theology too must frankly admit
that historically it knows nothing about the beginning of religion. The statements of the book of Genesis about a primordial
paradisiac state of the world and of man are meant to be, not
"recollections of primeval times," but a message in poetic form
about the greatness of the one Creator, about the essential
goodness of his creatures, about man's freedom, responsibility,
and sin. Serious theology today no longer has any difficulty in
accepting an evolution of the world and of man from lower
forms. Hence the interest of theology in the thesis of a "primitive monotheism" has perceptibly declined. In view of the state
of the sources, any attempt at a synthesis between the biblical
accounts and ethnological findings has become pointless. Fortunately, an easing of dogmatic restraints can be felt
everywhere, both on the part of theology and the Church and
on the part of ethnology and the science of religion.

Recent manuals on the history of religion often do not have a
chapter on a primordial or *the* primitive religion. Instead of
this we find one or mostly several chapters on *primitive religions*. It has even been suggested that we should begin quite
concretely, straightway, with Polynesian, North Indian, and
African religion; but such a procedure might lead us to overlook the common features which exist, despite everything, in

the different primitive religions.[33] At any rate the different cultures or, to use Ruth Benedict's term, "patterns of culture," must be understood in themselves[34] and the different religions in each case in the light of their own assumptions. Studies of religion today concentrate on this approach.

Religions are increasingly examined in their own specific forms by intensive field studies, with the aid of philology, psychology, sociology, ethnology, archaeology, history of art, and folklore. The "functionalistic" anthropology of Bronislaw Malinowski[35] has done a great deal to assist such field studies. It describes how the various institutions of a primitive culture "function," so that a viable whole emerges. When considered together, very odd and apparently pointless customs of the "primitives" have revealed their function. Hence the task of a modern science of religion is seen to consist, not in a priori constructions, not in classifying religions into "higher" and "lower," not in value judgments on particular religions, but in bringing out the diversities among all the similarities, in analyzing the functions perceptible against the mysterious background, in respecting the religions in all their diversity of experience.

Meanwhile all investigations have made one thing clear, that hitherto in the whole long history of mankind *no people or tribe* has ever been discovered *without any traces of religion.* Even in the case of Neanderthal man 100,000 years ago ideas of a future life are perceptible in his grave furnishings; and even

33. On these common features cf. V. Grønbach and J. Prytz Johansen, "Primitive Religion I–II" in *Handbuch der Religionsgeschichte,* edited by J. P. Asmussen and J. Lassøe in, in association with C. Colpe, vol. 1, Göttingen, 1971, pp. 11–151.

34. Cf. Ruth Benedict, *Patterns of Culture,* New York, 1948/London, 1949 (first published 1934).

35. Cf. Bronislaw Malinowski, *Magic, Science and Religion and Other Essays,* Beacon Press, Boston, 1948.

Heidelberg man 150,000 years ago appears to have offered a sacrifice of first fruits. Religion has always existed. Both historically and geographically religion is ubiquitous. In fact, in the study of the history of religion there has occurred what amounts to a reversal in the formulation of the problem. As Bronislaw Malinowski puts it:

> Tylor had still to refute the fallacy that there are primitive peoples without religion. Today we are somewhat perplexed by the discovery that to a savage all is religion, that he perpetually lives in a world of mysticism and ritualism. If religion is co-extensive with "life" and with "death" into the bargain, if it arises from all "collective" acts and from all "crises in the individual's existence," if it comprises all savage "theory" and covers all his "practical concerns"—we are led to ask, not without dismay: What remains outside it, what is the world of the "profane" in primitive life?[36]

Is it not clear why some of the authorities on the subject, precisely as a result of their understanding of the history of religion, maintain that religion will exist always. Is religion then an eternal yearning of mankind?

One of the most outstanding authorities of the present time on religion, Mircea Eliade, has expressed his surprise that Freud's *Totem and Taboo,* this *roman noir frénétique,* could have had such "incredible success" among Western intellectuals, although the leading ethnologists of Freud's own time— from W. H. Rivers and Franz Boas to A. L. Kroeber, Bronislaw Malinowski, and Wilhelm Schmidt—had proved "the absurdity of such a primordial 'totemic banquet.' "[37] It was in vain

36. Ibid., p. 7.
37. M. Eliade, "Cultural Fashions and the History of Religion" in J. M.

that all these scholars had brought out the fact that totemism was not found at the beginnings of religion, that it is not universal, and that not all peoples had passed through a totemistic phase; that, among the many hundreds of totemistic tribes, Frazer himself had found that only four were aware of a rite which resembled a ritual killing and eating of a "totem god"; that this rite, therefore, has nothing to do with the origin of sacrifice, since totemism does not occur in the oldest cultures.

According to Eliade, Freud's genius must not be judged according to the "horror stories" which are put forward in *Totem and Taboo* as objective historical facts. What is important is that psychoanalysis has once and for all won the battle against the older psychologists. Consequently, of course—and also for many other reasons—it became a "cultural fashion." And, because it was the fashion, Freudian ideology even in its uncertain elements was accepted as proved by the Western intelligentsia after 1920. But if we look into this "cultural fashion" precisely with the ways and means of psychoanalysis, according to Eliade:

> We can lay open some tragic secrets of the modern Western intellectual: for example, his profound dissatisfaction with the worn-out forms of historical Christianity and his desire to violently rid himself of his forefathers' faith, accompanied by a strange sense of guilt, as if he himself had killed a God in whom he could not believe but whose absence he could not bear. For this reason I have said that a cultural fashion is immensely significant, no matter what its objective value may be; the success of certain ideas or ideologies reveals to us the spiritual and existen-

Katagawa (ed.), *The History of Religions. Essays on the Problem of Understanding*, Chicago and London, 1967, p. 24.

tial situation of all those for whom these ideas or ideologies constitute a kind of soteriology.[38]

Religion—Merely Wishful Thinking?

Historically and biographically there can be no doubt that Freud was an atheist from his student years. He was an atheist long before he became a psychoanalyst. Consequently Freud's atheism was not grounded in his psychoanalysis, but preceded it. This too is what Freud constantly maintained, that psychoanalysis does not necessarily lead to atheism. It is a method of investigation and healing and can be practiced by both atheists and theists. And for that very reason Freud the atheist defends himself against the charge of extrapolating an atheistic Weltanschauung from a "neutral working tool." Methodological "atheism" must not be turned into ideological atheism, psychoanalysis cannot be made into a total explanation of reality.

Freud *took over from Feuerbach and his successors* the essential arguments for his personal atheism: "All I have done—and this is the only thing that is new in my exposition—is to add some psychological foundation to the criticisms of my great predecessors," says Freud both modestly and rightly.[39] Even Feuerbach had produced a psychological substantiation of atheism: wishes, fantasies, or the power of imagination are responsible for the projection of the idea of God and of the whole religious pseudo- or dream-world. Like Marx's opium theory at an earlier stage, Freud's illusion theory is grounded in Feuerbach's projection theory. What is essentially new is

38. Ibid., pp. 21–38; quotation, p. 25.
39. S. Freud, *Die Zukunft einer Illusion* in *Studienausgabe* 9:169. (*The Future of an Illusion* in *S.E.* 21 [1961]:35.)

merely Freud's psychoanalytical reinforcement of Feuerbach's theory.

This means, however, that for the critique of Freud's atheism as well the arguments that can be adduced against Feuerbach's (and Marx's) atheism, particularly against the evidence drawn from psychology and philosophy of religion, are valid. And insofar as Feuerbach's (and Marx's) atheism has turned out to be a hypothesis which in the last resort has not been conclusively proved, so too must Freud's atheism now, in the last resort, be seen as a *hypothesis which has not been conclusively proved.*

Of course, Freud had asked about the background of Feuerbach's psychological projection theory and applied the tests of depth psychology to its unconscious assumptions. Hence he was able to give greater depth to this hypothesis in the light of the history of religion and then of psychology of religion. But by this means Freud had no more provided an independent substantiation for the projection theory than Marx did. For Freud had *taken for granted* this projection theory (apparently irrefutably substantiated by his "great predecessors") and then had asked, and tried to show, how it could be explained in the light of the history of religion and the psychology of religion. And it is precisely this assumption which turns out in the last resort to be without foundation.

It is to Freud's immense credit that he worked out how much the unconscious determines the individual human being and the history of mankind, how fundamental are even the earliest childhood years, the first parent-child relationships, and the approach to sexuality for a person's religious attitudes and ideas as well. But we have to see very clearly in connection with Feuerbach, Marx, and Freud that from the indisputable influence of *psychological* (or economic and social) factors on religion and the idea of God no conclusions can be drawn about the existence or nonexistence of God.

We may put this in a more concrete summary form by referring to Freud's main statement on the critique of religion: "Religious ideas are fulfillments of the oldest, strongest, and most urgent wishes of mankind." This is quite true, as the believer in God can also say. And he will admit at the same time:

Religion, as Marx shows, can certainly be opium, a means of social assuagement and consolation (repression). But it need not be.

Religion, as Freud shows, can certainly be an illusion, the expression of a neurosis and psychological immaturity (regression). But it need not be.

All human believing, hoping, loving—related to a person, a thing, or God—certainly contains an element of projection. But its object need not, for that reason, be a mere projection.

Belief in God can certainly be very greatly influenced by the attitude of the child to its father. But this does not mean that God may not exist.

Consequently the problem does not lie in the fact that belief in God can be psychologically explained. It is not a question of a choice for or against psychology. From the psychological standpoint belief in God always exhibits the structure and content of a projection or can be under suspicion of being a mere projection. It is the same with lovers: every lover necessarily projects his own image of her on to the beloved. But does this mean that his beloved does not exist or at any rate does not exist substantially as he sees her and thinks of her? With the aid of his projections can he not even understand her more profoundly than someone who tries as a neutral observer to judge her from outside? The mere fact of projection, therefore, does

not decide the existence or nonexistence of the object to which
it refers.

It is at this point that the Freudian argument from the
abnormal to the normal, from the neurotic to the religious—
however well justified—finds its essential limitations. Is religion human *wishful thinking?* And must God for that reason
be merely a human wishful structure, an infantile illusion or
even a purely neurotic delusion? As we have argued elsewhere
against Feuerbach, a real God may certainly correspond to the
wish for God. This possibility is one which even Freud did not
exclude. And why should wishful thinking be entirely and
universally discredited? Is not wishing wholly and entirely
human, wishing in small matters or in great, wishing in regard
to the goods of this world, in regard to our fellowmen, to the
world, and perhaps also in regard to God?

Of course, religious belief would be in a bad way if there
were no genuine grounds for it or if no grounds remained after
a psychoanalytic treatment of the subject; however devout its
appearance, such a faith would be immature, infantile, and
perhaps even neurotic. But is a faith bad and its truth dubious
simply because—like psychoanalysis itself—it also involves all
possible instinctual motivations, lustful inclinations, psychodynamic mechanisms, conscious and unconscious desires?
Why in fact should I not be permitted to wish? Why should I
not be allowed to wish that the sweat, blood, and tears, all the
suffering of millennia, may not have been in vain, that definitive happiness may finally be possible for all men—especially
the despised and downtrodden? And why should I not on the
other hand feel an aversion to being required to be satisfied
with rare moments of happiness and—for the rest—to come to
terms with "normal unhappiness"? May I not too feel aversion
to the idea that the life of the individual and of mankind is
ruled only by pitiless laws of nature, by the play of chance and

by the survival of the fittest, and that all dying is a dying into nothingness?[40]

It does not follow—as some theologians have mistakenly concluded—from man's profound desire for God and eternal life that God exists and eternal life and happiness are real. But those atheists who think that what follows is the nonexistence of God and the unreality of eternal life are mistaken too. It is true that the wish alone does not contain within itself its fulfillment. It *may* be that nothing corresponds to the oldest, strongest, and most urgent wishes of mankind and that mankind has actually been cherishing illusions for millennia. Just like a child who in its solitude, forsakenness, distress, and need for happiness wishes wholeheartedly, longs, imagines, and fantasizes that it might have a father in some distant Russian camp, cherishes illusions, gives way to self-deception, pursues wish images, unless . . . unless? Unless the father, long assumed to be dead, whom the child knows only from hearsay, had by some chance remained alive and—although no one believed it any longer—still existed. Then—then indeed—the child would actually be right against the many who did not believe in the father's existence. Then there would in fact be a reality corresponding to the child's wishful thinking and one day perhaps it might be seen face to face.

Here, then, we have reached the crux of the problem, which is not at all difficult to understand and in the face of which any kind of projection theory, opium theory, or illusion theory momentarily loses its suggestive power. Perhaps this being of our longings and dreams does actually exist. Perhaps this being who promises us eternal bliss does exist. Not only the bliss of

40. Cf. A. Görres, "Alles spricht dafür, nichts Haltbares dagegen. Kritische Reflexionen eines Analytikers über den christlichen Glauben" in H. Zahrnt (ed.), *Jesus und Freud. Ein Symposium von Psychoanalytikern und Theologen*, Munich, 1972, pp. 36–52.

the baby at its mother's breast—which, according to Freud, permanently determines a person's unconscious—but a quite different reality in the future which corresponds to the unconscious and conscious aspirations precisely of the mature, adult human being and to which the oldest, strongest, most urgent wishes of mankind are oriented, which can fulfill our longing for infinite happiness. Perhaps. Who knows?

Freud's explanation of the psychological genesis of belief in God did not refute this faith itself. Freud analyzed and deduced these religious ideas psychologically. And this is precisely what theologians and churchmen should never have denied him or Feuerbach the right to do at an earlier stage. For it is possible and also legitimate to give a psychological interpretation of belief in God. But is the psychological aspect itself the whole of religion? It must be observed that Freud has not in fact destroyed and refuted religious ideas in principle and neither atheists nor theologians should ever have read this into Freud's critique of religion. For psychological interpretation alone, from its very nature, cannot penetrate to the absolutely final or first reality: as to what this reality is it remains neutral in principle. From the psychological standpoint—and even the positive force of the argument must not be overestimated—the existence of God must remain an open question.

Freud's atheism, of which he was quite certain long before any of his psychological discoveries, thus turns out to be a pure hypothesis, an unproved postulate, a dogmatic claim. And at bottom Freud was well aware of this. For religious ideas, though incredible, are for him also irrefutable. In principle they might also be true. Even for him, what has to be said of their psychological nature by no means decides their truth content and truth value. We have heard his answer: "We tell ourselves, it would indeed be fine . . . , but . . ."

Faith in Science

For Freud belief in God is replaced by belief in science, "our god logos,"[41] in which he finds the "sure support" which is "lacking" to believers in God.[42] We see how emphatically Freud, fully aware of the inadequacy of man and of his progress, nevertheless confessed his faith: "We believe that it is possible for scientific work to gain some knowledge about the reality of the world . . ."[43] And how emphatically he forswore unbelief: "No, our science is no illusion."[44]

Can faith in science replace faith in God? We cannot explain here what we would have to say about the modern ideal of knowledge, natural science, and the question of God; this position would certainly not be opposed to a critical rationality, but it would definitely be against an ideological rationalism. In any case, we have to draw attention to the fact that, contrary to Freud's prophecy, neither in the West nor in the East has belief in God yet disappeared to make way for science; particularly after the experience of National Socialism and of communism, modern atheism has lost much of its credibility. But for innumerable people throughout the world belief in God has gained a new future, particularly in our time. Both Feuerbach's anthropological atheism and Marx's social-political atheism, as well as Freud's psychoanalytical atheism, are still far from gaining universal acceptance. Freud's thesis, then, of the supersession of religion by science turns out to be an assertion without any apparent foundation: an extrapolation into the future which even today, in retrospect, cannot in any way be verified.

41. S. Freud, *Die Zukunft einer Illusion* in *Studienausgabe* 9:187. (*The Future of an Illusion* in *S.E.* 21 [1961]:54.)
42. Ibid. 9:188. (*S.E.* 21:54–55.)
43. Ibid. 9:188. (*S.E.* 21:54–55.)
44. Ibid. 9:189. (*S.E.* 21:56.)

On the other hand, for a long time we have ceased to take every advance in science—as was assumed in Freud's student years—as a contradiction to belief in God. And among natural scientists and psychologists also the question is asked whether the core of belief in God has really been affected by the progress of science up to now and by the corrections which were, to be sure, necessarily involved in it. Is there really an essential contradiction between science and belief in God?

Meanwhile, however, the very progress of science has involved it in a crisis far greater than what Freud—for all his skepticism in regard to progress—anticipated. The indubitable progress of science in all fields leads many today, particularly in industrial nations, to doubt this faith in science, which was held also by Freud—the belief that science, and the technology resulting from it, automatically implies progress and is thus the key to that universal happiness of mankind which, according to Freud, is not provided by religion. On the other hand, it is possible today to point to the ambivalent character of this progress of science and technology, which so easily evades any kind of human control and now spreads a fear of the future often amounting to apocalyptic terror.[45] Freud himself had only a limited confidence in progress. He was not certain of the future of our civilization; he regarded as highly dangerous the force of the death-instinct and the excessive accumulation of the potential of aggression. For him the struggle between reason and destruction was far from being decided.[46]

45. G. R. Taylor, *The Doomsday Book*, London, 1970; S. Kirban, *Die geplante Verwirrung*, Wetzlar, 1972; G. Ehrensvärd, *Nach uns die Steinzeit. Das Ende des technischen Zeitalters*, Bern, 1972; D. Widener, *Kein Platz für Menschen. Das programmierte Selbstmord*, Frankfurt, 1972; E. E. Snyder, *Todeskandidat Erde. Programmierter Selbstmord durch unkontrollierten Fortschritt*, Munich, 1972; M. Lohmann (ed.), *Gefährdete Zukunft*, Munich, 1973; H. Gruhl, *Ein Planet wird geplündert. Die Schreckensbilanz unserer Politik*, Frankfurt, 1976.
46. In this connection cf. S. Freud, *Das Unbehagen in der Kultur* (1930) in

The ideology which maintains that the progress of scientific development leads of itself to a more humane outlook has now been shattered anyway. This progress has been in many ways a destructive influence, a rationality bearing irrational features, a god "logos" which has increasingly turned out to be an idol. Scientists will still rightly insist on a continual concern for science and technology and consequently also for human progress in great things and in small. But even they think that belief in science as a total explanation of reality, as a Weltanschauung, must be abandoned. Technology must no longer be regarded as a substitute religion providing a cure for all evils. The euphoria of progress as an ideology must be abandoned; the illusion that everything can be planned, of total feasibility, must be given up. From this standpoint, for many people and even for many scientists, there arises a question which is the very opposite of the one that faced Freud: might not ethics and religion themselves prove helpful in the quest for a new synthesis between controlled technical progress and a human existence liberated from the pressures of progress? Such a synthesis would comprise not only a more just social structure, more humane working conditions, greater closeness to nature, but also the satisfaction of man's nonmaterial needs, those values, that is, which alone make human life worth living, which alone make it truly human.

Nevertheless, it would be wrong in principle to exploit the now widespread skepticism in regard to science and technology for theological advantage. Not every step away from scientific credulity is a step toward theistic piety. Skepticism toward science and technology is far from being a foundation for belief in God.

Theologians must recognize the fact that today there are

Studienausgabe 9:191–270. (Civilisation and Its Discontents in S.E. 21 [1961]: 56–145.)

many people who reject an ideologizing of science as a total explanation of reality, but who are equally skeptical when it comes to belief in God. There are today many people who no longer fight passionately for their atheistic convictions, but they are even less inclined to speak out passionately for a belief in God. Between skepticism and affirmation we now find all too often not indeed a militant atheism, but one that is practical, everyday, and banal.

Today there are only a few scientists who, like Freud, publicly acknowledge their unbelief. But neither are there too many who publicly bear witness to their belief. Religion, faith, God—for many, all this seems singularly faded, tobooed, left undecided; they remain uncommitted. Belief in God is regarded as a private affair which does not concern anyone else. As far as religion is concerned, is there not in many cases a widespread easygoing tolerance, leaving everyone to believe just what he happens to believe?

Can Religiosity Be Repressed?

It would certainly not be entirely irrelevant to raise the question whether we are perhaps faced here with a repression phenomenon which naturally has its own, and not least historical, roots? The unnecessary controversies, already mentioned, between Church and science explain at least up to a point why scientists today prefer to be silent rather than to speak of God. We have observed that sexuality can be repressed. Hence it is possible to ask if perhaps the future, fear and hope, the question of the meaning of life, even religiosity, can also be repressed. One should not appeal too quickly to objective science, to impartial reason. Even scientific reason can be corrupted, by all kinds of wishes, instincts, inclinations, childhood fixations, prejudices. And this occurs particularly at the point where it is not a question of "exact" (mathematical, scientific, technological, "pure") conclusions, but of their assumptions and applications, especially where the problems of one's own life are involved. Atheists accuse religion of being wishful thinking. But we for our part may ask whether atheism too might not be wishful thinking, projection. Raising the question is not, of course, the same thing as answering it.

For Freud personally, so far as this is of interest here, the problem becomes acute. Was there perhaps a repression problem involved in the atheism he maintained to the end? This closing question of the present critique, which we raise with the utmost caution, is not intended to be a final appeal to an interpretation in terms of individual psychology that would neutralize Freud's criticism of religion. Nevertheless, there is food for thought in the fact that—as we have seen—Freud was not brought up without religion. He has testified in his "An Autobiographical Study" to the fact that he was quite familiar with the Bible, but oddly enough in a sentence which was added only in 1935.[47] He also admits that he was seized in his early years by a strong bent toward speculation on the riddle of the world and of man, but again, oddly enough, he resisted this inclination: "As a young man I felt a strong attraction towards speculation and ruthlessly checked it."[48] Thus he "secretly nursed the hope" of arriving by a detour through physiology at his "original objective, philosophy." "For that was my original ambition, before I knew what I was intended to do in the world."[49] At the age of forty he wrote to his friend

47. S. Freud, "Selbstdarstellung" in I. Grubrich-Simitis (ed.), *Schriften zur Geschichte der Psychoanalyse*, Frankfurt, 1971, p. 40. ("An Autobiographical Study" in *S.E.* 20 [1959]:8.)

48. Cf. E. Jones, *Sigmund Freud* 1:32 f., 38, 67, 324, 327, 382, 421; 2:394.

49. S. Freud, "Brief an W. Fliess" 1.1.1896, in *Aus den Anfängen der Psychoanalyse*, p. 152. (English translation, *The Origins of Psycho-Analysis*, Imago Publishing Company, London, 1954, p. 141.)

Fliess about his yearning for knowledge: "As a young man my only longing was for philosophical knowledge, and now that I am changing over from medicine to psychology I am in the process of fulfilling this wish. I became a therapist against my will."[50]

Evidently the young Freud was preoccupied with questions which can be called philosophical, ideological, or religious. And evidently Freud in his old age—as he has told us himself, everything else in the meantime had been merely a "detour"—returned to the questions of his youth and became intensely occupied until his death mainly with problems of religion. In this respect from his youth onward and from his first biblical studies nothing fascinated him more than the "founder" of that religion—the Jewish—from which he came. As early as 1913, for three lonely September weeks, he stood every day contemplating the statue of Moses by Michelangelo in San Pietro in Vincoli in Rome, in order to write his early (anonymously published) work on this figure. And he also wrote the last great work of his life on the history and significance of this same Moses. What was the source of this fascination?

Undoubtedly Freud is one of the great moralists of mankind. He was not at all a sexual libertine as many thought at the time and as some maintain even today. In his whole way of life and in his sexual life in particular he observed an extremely strict morality. In fact he was not without a deep-rooted prudery and his morality displays some very strict, even legalistic, sombre features.

His theory of man had nothing to do with "pansexualism" or

---

50. S. Freud, "Brief an W. Fliess" 2.4.1896, in S. Freud, *Briefe 1873–1939*, edited by E. L. Freud, Frankfurt, 1960, p. 227. (English translation, *Letters of Sigmund Freud, 1873–1939*, edited by Ernest L. Freud, Hogarth Press, London, 1961, p. 241.)

"making the most of one's instincts." On the contrary, for Freud, all human civilization rested essentially on the renunciation of instinct, on subduing the infantile pleasure principle in favor of the reality principle. There is little mention in his work of either "joy" or "beauty." It is noticeable that the ethical requirements, which he wanted to see substantiated purely rationally, without the aid of religion, were identical in content with those of the Mosaic decalogue. And it can scarcely be doubted that, while he speaks himself of the strict education which made its mark on his childhood and in which a father complex had been observed as a result of his self-analysis, he had remained unconsciously indebted to the ancient Mosaic legalism.

His atheism, on the other hand, is not original, but—as we saw very clearly—adopted, not connected with the psychoanalytical method, which he developed under the enormous influence of supposedly atheistic natural science, at this time replacing for him the Jewish belief in God. Belief in God, however, was not simply replaced by scientific arguments, but by another faith, the quasi-religious faith in science. For Freud personally, then, psychoanalysis too is far more than merely a method of research and healing; it is the basis of an atheistic Weltanschauung, a kind of substitute for religion.

At the same time it is striking that Freud's atheism in particular was not shared by many of his friends, even though they shared with him important convictions in the field of depth psychology. And also many of his own students, who adopted his psychoanalytical method in its entirety, did not, as he himself admits, adopt his atheism. Thus Freud's atheism remains for him a wholly personal basic attitude and has nothing to do with psychoanalysis as such. Is it not perhaps possible that we are faced here with the phenomenon of a Jewish religiosity repressed for reasons that can be understood?

We need not settle the question here. In any case we have the greatest respect for the life and work of this singularly consistent scholar. We have the greatest respect too for his long-drawn-out death. Death released him from a cruel suffering which he had endured for years: a cancer of the palate, borne for sixteen years with heroic equanimity and necessitating more than thirty operations.

But his death itself raises questions, the death of this man to whom his family doctor of his last ten years dedicated his recollections.[51] We see with astonishment the powerful, emotionally charged role which death played for this man with his austere science and absolutely clear rationality. He had wrestled with this problem throughout his life and had not mastered it even at the end. It began with an almost obsessive "preoccupation with the prospective dates of his death";[52] it was nourished from sources in Jewish superstitions about "attacks of fear of death,"[53] particularly in connection with his fifty-first year; and it continued to his feeling of the "guilt of the survivor" at his father's death.[54] All this belongs to the very personal background of someone who finally saw the whole reality of man as marked by the mutual antagonism of the instincts of Eros and Thanatos, the life- and death-instincts.

Unbroken, despite all his suffering, Freud continued to work to the end. In 1938 the invasion of Austria by the National Socialists forced him to leave Vienna and emigrate to London. But his illness followed its inexorable course. At the end of August 1939 the cancer had eaten a way through from the mouth cavity to outside. A mosquito net had to be stretched

51. Max Schur, *Freud: Living and Dying*, Hogarth Press and Institute of Psycho-Analysis, London, 1972.
52. Ibid., p. 26.
53. Ibid., p. 98.
54. Ibid., p. 109.

over his bed because the smell attracted flies. The war had begun and Freud heard the first air-raid warnings. Aged eighty-three, he died on 23 September 1939, at three o'clock in the morning, after the family doctor, with his consent, had eased his passing with an injection of morphia. As early as 1915 Freud had written in his "Thoughts for the Times on War and Death": "Towards the actual person who has died we adopt a special attitude: something like admiration for some-one who has accomplished a very difficult task."[55]

55. Ibid., p. 529.

CRITIQUE OF THE CRITIQUE

4

Freud's atheism seems to be no better substantiated than that of Feuerbach and Marx. But does this mean that his critique of religion can therefore be dismissed? Again, no more than that of Feuerbach and Marx. This critique too must be understood less as an interim stage to be quickly passed through than as a warning shadow constantly accompanying belief in God. The much-quoted "revolution of psychoanalysis," Freud's inspired discovery and methodical scientific probing of the dynamic reality of the unconscious, has had lasting effects also on religion and belief in God. Whatever may be thought of individual elements of the psychoanalytical theory, which he later continued to improve and modify empirically and conceptually, from Freud onward all that is human, all man's conscious individual and social activity, even his religion and his belief in God, must be seen as essentially connected with that region of the psyche which has its own laws and yet remains beyond deliberate control and direct observation: the unconscious, the deepest stratum in man.

Honesty in Dealing with Religion

"He [Freud] has already reinforced the belief of unbelievers; he has scarcely begun to purify the faith of believers," says the French philosopher Paul Ricoeur.[1] Theologians can learn from Freud; his critical writings on religion amount to a single plea for *honesty in dealing with religion*. In this respect "people are guilty of every possible sort of dishonesty and intellectual misdemeanor. Philosophers (and, I might add, theologians) stretch the meaning of words until they retain scarcely any-

1. Paul Ricoeur, "The Atheism of Freudian Psychoanalysis" in *Concilium*, June 1966 (vol. 6, no. 2), pp. 31–37. Quotation, p. 36.

thing of the original sense."[2] There are those who "give the name of 'God" to some vague abstraction which they have created for themselves."[3] Or they "persist in describing as 'deeply religious' anyone who admits to a sense of man's insignificance or impotence in the face of the universe."[4] Freud himself in any case professes atheism unequivocally and, in his sincere critical attitude to religion, is prepared to allow also for the most "disagreeable reproaches." "If a man has already learnt in his youth to rise superior to the disapproval of his contemporaries, what can it matter to him in his old age when he is certain soon to be beyond the reach of all favour or disfavour."[5]

More is involved, however, than mere intellectual probity; it is a question of *critical rationality.* Certainly there can be no belief in science in the sense of a reason made absolute; this objection in the spirit of Pascal had to be raised against Freud. But on the other hand there must be no skepticism in regard to science in the sense of making faith an absolute; this must be said in the spirit of Descartes *for* Freud. For we can see in connection with Pascal, Jansenism, Kierkegaard, and Barth how often Christians and theologians have been in danger of devaluing the conclusions of reason, in order to revalue faith—a specific form of hostility to reason which does not seem in any way to be required by Christian faith. Must we cease to be philosophers and scholars in order truly to believe in God? Did not Pascal, Kierkegaard, and Barth allow faith to overwhelm reason in this way? Did they not in practice make Christian revelation the unique source of truth and certainty?

2. S. Freud, *Die Zukunft einer Illusion* in *Studienausgabe* 9:166. (*The Future of an Illusion* in *S.E.* 21 [1961]:12.)
  3. Ibid. 9:166. (*S.E.* 21:12.)
  4. Ibid. 9:167. (*S.E.* 21:32.)
  5. Ibid. 9:170. (*S.E.* 21:36.)

Against all Protestant biblicism and Catholic traditionalism, therefore, must not a radical correction of their course be required from Church and theology? Instead of hostile polemical mutual opposition, or even agreement to differ while maintaining peaceful coexistence, must there not now be a critical and dialogic cooperation between theology and science, particularly between theology and natural science? Consequently, all that can be said, in principle, from the standpoint of Descartes and the tradition he represents for the modern ideal of knowledge, for natural science and the new setting of the problem of God, and in general for a critical rationality without ideological rationalism—for the most part all this amounts to a justification of Freud's method of psychology oriented to natural science.

In any case Freud was decidedly right to object to the idea of *Credo quia absurdum,* as if religious doctrines were entirely above reason and wholly beyond its claims. As if their truth needed only to be inwardly perceived and not understood. He calls such a *Credo* "an authoritative statement" without "binding force" and goes on to ask: "Am I obliged to believe *every* absurdity? And if not, why this one in particular?"[6] There is no appeal to an authority above reason: "If the truth of religious doctrines is dependent on inner experience which bears witness to that truth, what is one to do about the many people who do not have this rare experience? One may require every man to use the gift of reason which he possesses, but one cannot erect, on the basis of a motive that exists only for a very few, an obligation that shall apply to everyone."[7]

Freud rightly objects to the widespread attitude or philosophy of "as if," which means that the groundlessness, even the

6. S. Freud, *Die Zukunft einer Illusion* in *Studienausgabe* 9:162. (*S.E.* 21:28.)
7. Ibid. 9:162. (*S.E.* 21:28.)

absurdity, of religious doctrines is perhaps appreciated, "but for a variety of practical reasons we have to behave 'as if' we believed in these fictions."[8] We practice a religious conformism or opportunism mainly because of the incomparable importance of religion "for the maintenance of human society."[9] To a person not corrupted by such a philosophy religion would seem to be disposed of as soon as its absurdity and irrationality have been recognized: "It cannot be expected of him that precisely in treating his most important interests he shall forgo the guarantees he requires for all his ordinary activities."[10] Even children, if they were more rational, would listen to a fairy story and then raise the question: "Is that true?"

Justification of Freud's Critique of Religion

But, over and above the general requirement of intellectual honesty and critical rationality, it must be said that the *relative justification of Freud's specific critique of religion* can no more be disputed than that of similar attempts on the part of Feuerbach and Marx. What Feuerbach wanted from the philosophical standpoint and Marx from the political-social, Freud sought from the standpoint of depth psychology: emancipation, comprehensive liberation, more humanity on the part of man. It meant in particular opposition to tutelage, domination, oppression by religion, Church, God himself. Was all this entirely wrong? To bring out its concrete meaning, a few points may be mentioned here—which incidentally can be substantiated also from Adler or Jung.

Freud rightly criticizes defective *forms of religion.* Christians should admit in a spirit of self-criticism:

8. Ibid. 9:162. (*S.E.* 21:28.)
9. Ibid. 9:162. (*S.E.* 21:28–29.)
10. Ibid. 9:163. (*S.E.* 21:29.)

When religion is completely concentrated on the "wholly Other," contact with reality is inevitably lost. Religious questions thus easily become a form of self-deception and escapism. Religion becomes an infantile commitment, without regard to reality, to a tyrannical superego; God becomes a displacement-substitute.

When religion relies solely on wish-fulfillment and not on intrinsic truth, it is reduced to pure satisfaction of needs. Such a religion is unquestionably a return to infantile structures, a regression to childish wishing.

When religion is manifested in rigid fidelity to the letter, in a legalistic conscience, in obsessive, pedantic and petty repetition of certain prayers, formulas, and rituals, religious ideas come close to delusive fabrications, religious observances to substitute satisfaction resulting from obsessive cultic repetition. Such religious practices, which have become pointless or inadequately motivated, are often defensive and protective measures dictated by fear, guilt feelings, and tormented conscience, against certain—often unconscious—temptations and threatening punishments, just like the private ritual (for example, ablutomania), of the obsessional neurotic.

Freud also rightly criticizes *the churches' misuse of power*. The facts are well known:

How abundant are the examples of arrogance of power and misuse of power in the history of the churches: intolerance and cruelty toward deviationists, crusades, inquisition, extermination of heretics, obsession with witches, struggle against theological research, oppression of their own theologians— right up to the present time.

How over the centuries the churches have acted like a superego: dominating souls in the name of God, exploiting the dependence and immaturity of poor sinners, requiring submission to the taboos of untested authority, continually repressing sexuality and displaying contempt for women (in the law of celibacy, in excluding women from church ministries). What a heap of *ecclesiogenic neuroses:* neuroses that result from the constraints of the ecclesiastical system, clerical domination, confessional practice, sexual repression, hostility to progress and to science. There is no need to reopen here the *chronique scandaleuse* of Christianity and the churches.[11]

Freud rightly criticizes, finally, the *traditional image of God.* People are still too little aware of some of the ways in which it has been formed.

Often enough a believer's image of God springs, not from original insight and free decision, but from an *image of a vindictive or kind father* imprinted at an early age.

Often enough early childhood experiences with adults who appear as "gods" are *transferred* both positively and negatively *to God,* so that behind the image of God the image of one's own father becomes visible, even though the latter has long been forgotten or repressed (it is the same with the mother image as reflected in the Mother of God or in Mother Church).

Often enough the vindictive Father-God is deliberately *misused* by parents *as a means of education,* in order to discipline their children, with long-term negative consequences for the religious attitudes of those children as they grow up.

Often enough *religion and sexuality* (the latter frequently repressed by religion), are knit together from the very beginning in such a way that what appear to be religious conflicts are really only fixations on the earliest experiences of the family-scene.

11. Cf. H. Küng, *Christ sein,* Munich, 1974, D I: "Die Praxis der Kirche." (English translation, *On Being a Christian,* New York, 1976/London, 1977, D I: "The Practice of the Church.")

The Importance of Psychotherapy for Religion

In his critical analysis, in both theory and practice, Freud cultivated a brilliant artistic style and made use of all the *possibilities of language.* This can be seen under three aspects:[12]

Stylistic-aesthetic: Using a style midway between the passionate and the prosaic, he gives the most emphatic expression to his interests and views.

Heuristic: proverbs, common phrases, "transparent words" are used to make the speaker conscious of what have hitherto been unconscious, buried planes of meaning.

Therapeutic: In the cooperation between patient and therapist language is almost the sole or at least the fundamental therapeutic tool. For language is the "phenomenon of consciousness which is constitutive for 'becoming man.' . . . Language makes man possible."[13] Not only man's ego, however, but also his superego, is linguistically structured, formed by the acquisition of language in internalizing speech patterns already existing and largely represented by the parents. "For it is worth noting that we understand what we call 'conscience'—so to speak—vocally-acoustically, as analogous to speech: it seems like a voice speaking to us within us and even as the voice of another person, a stranger in ourselves."[14] Language has, finally, a meaning also for the third, unconscious factor of the psyche, the id. Language plays a decisive role in all dreamwork and consequently in all rendering conscious and process-

---

12. H. M. Gauger, "Sprache und Sprechen im Werk Sigmund Freuds" in *Neue Rundschau* 85 (1974):568–90.

13. Ibid. 85:577.

14. Ibid. 85:582.

ing of repressions. For Freud the conscious ego comes to be from the unconscious id by a linguistic process.

Ought not theologians particularly and those engaged in pastoral practice, who *ex professo* have to deal with the "word," to learn from Freud the complex significance of language for preaching, discussion, exhortation, confession of sin or faith—language as a liberating, consoling, meaning-endowing power which can help both self-understanding and the understanding of others, both self-acceptance and the acceptance of others?

Psychologists and theologians, "doctors of souls" and pastors, have every reason today to enter into close cooperation. Fortunately both sides have made considerable progress in this respect.

Psychoanalysts today increasingly criticize the relegation of psychoanalysis to the realm of the natural sciences. This criticism is voiced, not only by those who follow the more recent political, social-critical trend, but also by those who adopt the orthodox individual-psychological approach. They recognize, in addition to the sexual, numerous intellectual and even religious impulses, queries, problems, which are not to be repressed but must be admitted.

But theologians and pastors are increasingly discovering today the critical potential of psychoanalysis for Church and theology. They recognize psychoanalysis, not only as a useful aid to the Church, but as an independent critical authority to which theology must render an account of the reality reference of many of its statements, an account which can make an effective contribution to a faith that is no longer infantile but adult. It will also clarify the content of faith, notably such important concepts as sin and guilt, justification and forgiveness, corporality and sexuality.

According to Freud, man should become aware of himself

by learning to control his instincts, bear the burden of his history, and master the problem of his sense of guilt. Involved in the "reality principle" is an ethical appeal, which coincides also with the great humane intentions of the Christian faith. Thus the discussion with Freud turns out to be a demand on the Christian understanding of man to see him also in his psychological reality as a free, mature, realistic, and assured person, for whom everything depends on learning to accept himself, coming to terms with the truth of his past, looking for the cause of his failure and sin and mastering them. In this way Christian faith and psychoanalysis might become partners in pursuit of the same humane goal.

Nevertheless, the *limitations* must be observed. The competence of psychoanalysis remains restricted to the field of psychological reality. Psychoanalysis, therefore, may not reduce all reality to the psychological sphere, if it is to avoid the danger of a "reductionist hermeneutic."[15] Psychoanalysis can remove neurotic guilt feelings, but it cannot liberate a person from real sin. It can eliminate psychosomatic illnesses, but it cannot answer ultimate questions about meaning and meaninglessness, life and death. Its aim is to bring things into consciousness, not to forgive; it is healing, not salvation.

Of course the ultimate questions call for an answer, to satisfy both the sick and the healthy. The problems of neuroses are themselves often linked with more fundamental problems of life and sometimes lead patients to ask what is the point of a cure. A psychoanalysis which is not merely skeptically and resignedly backward-looking, but progressively and communicatively forward-looking, will not be able simply to suppress the question of the meaning of life and also of suffering

15. Cf. Paul Ricoeur, "Atheism of Freudian Psychoanalysis," *Concilium*, vol. 6, no. 2, p. 31.

and dying. But the psychotherapist must then know that he will be able to answer such questions, which concern man as a whole, only if he deliberately goes beyond the limits of his science and appeals to some sort of religious or nonreligious faith.

The theologian for his part will have to be reserved in regard to psychological questions. He is not an expert and simply not equipped to be an arbitrator in the different psychotherapeutical controversies. He should not seek to judge theories which belong strictly to the field of psychology, but he should certainly take note of the problems associated with psychological theories which are relevant to religion. Nor, of course, can he escape the arduous task of examining certain conclusions of psychoanalysts and the criticism of their opponents from the standpoint of religion.[16]

Critique and Anticritique

Is one-sidedness the price of genius? Some apparently exaggerated views of Freud, which he links with his psychoanalytical theory, may be of a personal character and are perhaps founded in his own psychological development. But even if in practice he is often very dogmatic and unwilling to make formal corrections and even if he neglects or depreciates what is opposed to his teaching, he is right in his positive claims. This may be briefly illustrated by some points which are important also for religion and for religious attitudes.

16. Cf. E. Wiesenhütter, *Freud und seine Kritiker*, Darmstadt, 1974. The author provides a comprehensive survey of the criticism of Freud on the part of four groups: psychotherapists, psychiatrists, scholars in the field of the humanities, theologians. A useful survey of the theological reactions to Freud is provided by P. Homans, *Theology after Freud. An Interpretative Inquiry*, Indianapolis and New York, 1970, especially the chapters on R. Niebuhr and P. Tillich. See also N. O. Brown, D. Bakan, P. Rieff.

a. The critics assert that Freud overextended the concept of libido and, regardless of the differences, stretched it indiscriminately and mechanically to all possible expressions, not only of sexuality, but also of sympathy, of friendship, of parental, filial, and self love, and of religiosity, with the result that sexuality seemed to be everywhere present and everywhere active.

The objection which is raised against Freud's view is that sexuality can scarcely be granted such psychological universality. Other instinctual and personality factors, the whole complexity and multiple polarity of the instinctual and personality structure, need to be considered. Even with the small child, sucking, eating, and running produce pleasure, but these feelings of pleasure are not sexual in character. Sexual themes can be perceived everywhere in dream symbolism only if they are seen from the outset against a sexual background. Not everything that is forgotten is also repressed, not every slip is Freudian. Dreams are far from being always fulfillments of unfulfillable wishes. Behind them lie, not only sexual wishes, but a broad spectrum of emotions, affections, moods, sensations, instincts, and images as equally important themes which are not open to any systematic interpretation. Dream material consists of the problems left over from daily life, of feelings unsatisfied in daily life. Sexuality and love, sexual charm and personal charm, although often linked, must be distinguished in principle. The transference of theories of natural science, of physiology and brain mechanism, to mental happenings, which are seen as the functioning of a reflex machinery, reaches its limits at the point where what is involved are specifically human needs, which transcend all physiologically programmed instincts.

Nevertheless, it remains true that man in his whole conscious life—including his religious life—is continually determined in a decisive way by unconscious but very powerful experiences and recollections, data and tendencies, and psychological factors, among which sexuality has a primary role, all pressing into the light of consciousness. Disturbed sexuality is the cause of many neuroses which also find religious expression (for example, pathological scrupulosity, aggressiveness, sanctimoniousness and fanaticism). Sexuality acquires a truly ubiquitous virulence if it is not processed and integrated into the personality structure.

b. Critics assert that Freud exaggerated the experiential and environmental factors of early childhood by comparison with the innate dispositions (genetic constitution, influences in the mother's womb and in the process of birth).

The objection raised at this point is that an exclusive significance can scarcely be attributed to sexually determined childhood traumata. The significance of traumatizations and aberrations in early childhood should not be exaggerated; the conflicts of puberty, on the other hand, which are decisive for the formation of the adult, must not be underestimated. As early childhood sexual interest, which is not oriented expressly to any immediate sexual goal, and adult sexuality are qualitatively different, so too there are other conflicts at later stages of development which cannot simply be reduced to early childhood experiential and environmental factors. Dreams process what are predominantly current happenings and material and not merely those which go back to early childhood.

Nevertheless it cannot be disputed that, in addition to all the contents repressed later for a variety of reasons (conscience, environment, authority), there are instinctual wishes and conflicts from early childhood which determine a person's thinking, feeling, willing, and acting, and also his religious attitudes. Only too often the decisive problems and difficulties of a whole life result from the unprocessed events of early childhood, even though the person concerned is unaware of the fact.

c. The critics assert that a normally functioning sexual life does not exclude neurotic disorders which may be due to nonsexual causes. Consequently the free operation of sexuality is just as likely as its repression to produce conflicts in a person. Even psychoanalytic treatment can have negative consequences: insecurity in instinctual behavior, disorders in the sense of discretion, unresolved transferences, especially in analyses continued over years (fixation on the person of the doctor), complete relativization of ethical values, and dogmatic rigidity.

The objection which is raised is that Freudian therapy can scarcely be regarded as the only possible method of mastering mental conflicts. The positive vital, ethical, even religious objectives cannot be neglected and there must be an appeal to consciousness, responsibility, and will. A gradually increasing cooperation on the part of the patient and reciprocal discussion should be sought and a shortening of the treatment (which is otherwise available only to the rich) made possible (short-term therapy for the numerous current problems and neuroses which are not deep-rooted, a call for group therapy). Some rightly ask for a synthetic-intuitive approach to supplement the analytical-dissecting operation, for self-discovery, for the reconstruction of an integrated personality, and for arousing productive forces and trends so that the person may again find his way in life and become integrated into society (psychosynthesis, psychagogy).[17] This means prospective orientation, directed not merely backward but forward, in which the

17. Cf. P. Bjerre, *Psychosynthese*, Stuttgart, 1971; A. Maeder, "Psychosynthese-Psychogogik" in *Handbuch der Neurosenlehre und Psychotherapie*, vol. 3, Munich and Berlin, 1959, pp. 391–412.

psychotherapist's positive view of life—acting as partner to the discussion—plays a major part. Religion can be extremely important at this point.

Nevertheless, it must not be overlooked that an education that aims to instill absolute sincerity where sexuality is concerned is also important, particularly for morality. "Know thyself" can become the basis of the reconstruction of the personality. If certain conflicts are solved, this does not mean that their source can be ignored. With conflicts which emerge as a result of compromises between unconscious instinctual wishes or between conscious and unconscious (rejected and disguised, but half-accepted instinctual wishes), a more mature solution of the conflict must be brought about by rendering conscious the unconscious motivations. The patient should either learn to satisfy in reality the repressed impulses (including those which are sexual in origin) or—if they cannot be satisfied—to sublimate them; or he might even renounce satisfaction more successfully than before, so that the symptoms of his illness disappear and the way is laid open to new development and the full use of his vital energies.

d. The critics assert that the Oedipus complex on the man's part and, correspondingly, the castration complex on the woman's part have not been shown clinically, ontogenetically, or phylogenetically to be universal phenomena.

The objection which is raised is that an incestuous tie with the parents has never been shown either by ethnologists or psychologists to have been a normal occurrence in childhood. There is no evidence of the existence as a general rule of positive sexual ties to the parent of the opposite sex or of jealousy toward the parent of the same sex. The decisive factor in the production of neuroses is not so much the child's pleasure-seeking as those adverse conditions which give it the feeling of insecurity, helplessness, and defenselessness. Sexual difficulties often turn out to be more the effect than the cause of the neurotic constitution. Fixations of incestuous childhood relationships, therefore, should not be generalized and distorted into a crude sexual form. We must not simply impose a dogmatic, preconceived scheme on all possible observations and facts.

Nevertheless, it remains true that Freud's theories of the Oedipus or castration complex brought to light material which is important for all human conflicts. Feelings and affections for the people with whom the child enters into a relationship at an early—still more the earliest—stage (mother and father) are and remain of fundamental importance for a person's whole life. In view of what has to be said at a later stage, a brief critical comment on this point may be in place here. Does not the Oedipus complex too need demythologizing, and not merely in the light of the history of religion? It is not, of course, to be eliminated, but it certainly needs intelligent interpretation.

Literally understood, the Oedipus complex seems like a myth to many psychologists. And it is impossible a priori to deny what A. Hoche, the dream researcher, speaking perhaps for many others, expresses humorously if a little one-sidedly:

> The procedure of the psychoanalysts, who discover in their cases what dogma has projected into them, reminds me of the fathers who pretend to their children that they are surprised and pleased to find the Easter eggs which they themselves have hidden. . . . It is strange that, after sincerely trying for many years, I have not yet succeeded in finding anyone who desired his mother and wanted to kill his father. Other experienced colleagues have fared no better. The Oedipus complex travels around in literature

like the Flying Dutchman on the high seas: everyone talks about him, some believe in him, but no one has seen him.[18]

Nevertheless, if it is demythologized, the Oedipus complex expresses a truth. In connection with Freud's famous *Three Essays on the Theory of Sexuality*, psychoanalysts tried to investigate closely the very early development processes in the small human child, the "emergence of the first objective relationships," both by reconstruction on the basis of an analysis of later phases and by direct observation of children. Alongside the innate dispositions, the first objective relationship—that is, the relationship of the newborn child to its *mother* or her substitute—is of fundamental importance for the development of the personality: "For the new-born, the surround consists, so to say, of one single individual, the mother or her substitute."[19] The infant spends the first year of its life in union, in symbiosis, with the mother, in a "closed system" so to speak (dyad).

The appearance of a second relationship, however—normally with the *father*—is no less important. For it is through him that the tripolar child-parents relationship emerges. The "closed" mother-child relationship is opened; the symbiotic relationship situation is expanded to a community of three in which competition and conflict play an important part. And whether we call the conflict within this *three-person relationship* "Oedipus complex" or not, it is impossible to dispute the existence of the essential objective content of this term: "What takes place in the period of the Oedipus complex

18. A. Hoche, *Zentralblatt für die gesamte Neurologie und Psychiatrie* 55 (1930):206.
19. R. A. Spitz, *La première année de la vie de l'enfant*, Paris, 1959. (English translation, R. A. Spitz and G. W. Cobliner, *The First Year of Life: A Psychoanalytic Study of Normal and Deviant Development of Object Relations*, International Universities Press, New York, 1965, reprinted 1973, p. 13.)

(from the second to the sixth year of life), between these three persons, as experienced and mastered by the growing child, contributes decisively to character-formation. In other words, the definitive foundations of all later modes of feeling, thinking, and action are laid down during this period. . . . If the experiences of the Oedipus phase are not mastered, then neurotic symptoms are later practically the rule."[20]

Is all this not very important for the psychological understanding of religion? We must not lose sight, in particular, of this last group of problems. But, on the other hand, might not religion be very important for psychotherapy too?

The Importance of Religion for Psychotherapy

For Freud religion still had the function of a "universal obsessional neurosis." For Jung, on the other hand, it was precisely the want of religion, however this might be understood, which was the cause of many neuroses. It seemed to him that, "side by side with the decline of religious life, the neuroses grow noticeably more frequent."[21] For Freud, then, religion produced neuroses and was itself a neurosis substitute, but for Jung it produced a cure for neurosis and prevented the rise of neuroses. Jung had observed: "Among all my patients in the second half of life—that is to say, over thirty-five—there has not been one whose problem in the last resort was not that of finding a religious outlook on life. It is safe to say that everyone of them fell ill because he had lost what the living religions of

20. W. Loch, *Zur Theorie, Technik, und Therapie der Psychoanalyse*, Frankfurt, 1972, p. 142.
21. C. G. Jung, "Über die Beziehung der Psychotherapie zur Seelsorge" (1932) in *Psychologie und Religion*, Olten, 1971, pp. 129–52. Quotation, p. 139. (English translation, "Psychotherapists or the Clergy" pp. 327–47 of *Psychology and Religion: West and East*, vol. 11 of *Collected Works*, quotation, p. 335.)

every age have given to their followers, and none of them has been really healed who did not regain his religious outlook. This of course has nothing to do with a particular creed or membership of a church."[22]

What must be settled is not only the organization of the instincts, but also the question of the meaning of life. Jung sees in the psychoneurosis, in the last resort, "the suffering of a soul which has not discovered its meaning."[23] But what will happen when someone "has *no love*, but only sexuality; *no faith*, because he is afraid to grope in the dark; *no hope*, because he is disillusioned by the world and by life; and *no understanding*, because he has failed to read the meaning of his own existence?"[24] Here, according to Jung, is revealed a complex of problems which we simply cannot take too seriously and which brings the doctor of souls into the closest contact with the pastor. Here it is not only a question of repressed sexuality, even if the sexual sphere is in fact disturbed. Here it is a question of the meaning of life, by comparison with which the disturbance of the instinctual sphere may be secondary. "That is why I regard the religious problems which the patient puts before me as authentic and as possible causes of the neurosis."[25]

It is at the same time of central importance—so to speak, "the essence of the moral problem and the acid test of one's whole outlook on life"[26]—that a person should learn to accept himself, to accept himself with his darker side, with all the irrational, meaningless, evil elements. But at this very point it is not sufficient, with Freud, to make the darker side and the

22. Ibid., p. 138. (English translation, ibid. 11:334.)
23. Ibid., p. 134. (English translation, ibid. 11:330–31.)
24. Ibid., p. 135. (English translation, ibid. 11:331.)
25. Ibid., p. 142. (English translation, ibid. 11:338.)
26. Ibid., p. 143. (English translation, ibid. 11:339.)

evil elements conscious through psychoanalysis: "Freud has unfortunately overlooked the fact that man has never yet been able single-handed to hold his own against the powers of darkness—that is, of the unconscious. Man has always stood in need of the spiritual help which his particular religion held out to him. . . . Man is never helped in his suffering by what he thinks of for himself: only suprahuman, revealed truth lifts him out of his distress."[27]

Erich Fromm,[28] the German-American psychoanalyst, of Jewish descent, born in 1900 in Frankfurt am Main, attaches more importance than Freud and Jung to the fact that man must be seen, not merely abstractly or in the inner workings of his mind, as *homo psychologicus*, but—as Adler also sees him—in his essential relatedness to the world and thus increasingly—as the young Marx saw him—in his social-psychological and sociological dimension. Freud and Marx should be considered together: it becomes increasingly clear that this is Fromm's concern.[29] For man's passions cannot be derived directly and solely from biologically preexisting instincts; they are formed socio-biologically from the setting of the relationship of human needs to the environment and are thus essentially the consequence of social and cultural conditions.

The psychoanalyst himself is also involved in this relation-

27. Ibid., p. 148. (English translation, ibid. 11:344.)
28. Erich Fromm's *Psychoanalysis and Religion*, New Haven, Yale University Press, 1950, is fundamental to our themes. But cf. also Fromm's later work for the development in his attitude to religion: *The Sane Society*, Holt, Rinehart & Winston, New York, 1955/Routledge and Kegan Paul, London, 1956; *The Dogma of Christ and Other Essays on Religion, Psychology and Culture*, Holt, Rinehart and Winston, New York, 1963; *You Shall Be as Gods. A Radical Interpretation of the Old Testament and Its Tradition*, Holt, Rinehart and Winston, New York, 1966/Jonathan Cape, London, 1967.
29. Erich Fromm, *The Crisis of Psychoanalysis. Essays on Freud, Marx and Social Psychology*, Jonathan Cape, 1971.

ship to the world. His thinking and feeling are influenced by his Weltanschauung and his system of values. His interpretations differ according to the kind of person he is. Two basic attitudes must be observed here.[30] There are psychoanalysts who act as "adjustment advisers": for them the primary goal of life and also of psychoanalysis is "social adjustment," adaptation to the existing social structures. Other psychoanalysts regard themselves as true "doctors of souls": for them the primary goal is the "cure of the soul," that is, the optimal development of a person's potentialities, the realization of his individuality and of his moral and intellectual integrity in the unfolding of a fruitful affirmation of life and of love.

Starting out in this way, how does Fromm see religion? He makes this clear in his lectures *Psychoanalysis and Religion*, which represent a consistent continuation of his work on the psychology of ethics.[31] Psychoanalysis, he maintains, which is concerned with human individuality and integrity, is by no means irreconcilably opposed to a genuine humanitarian (not authoritarian), religion.[32] For such a humanitarian religion is certainly not simply to be derived from a supernatural power to which man has to submit. Absolutely speaking, it does not need a God beyond this world on whom alone the acceptance of life could be based. But neither is it simply to be traced—as Freud traced it—to a superego, a supposedly authoritarian conscience. As if conscience could not also provide a balance and be a calming influence; as if it could not help man to overcome estrangement and lack of identity. On the contrary,

30. Erich Fromm, *Psychoanalysis and Religion*, chap. 4: "The Psychoanalyst as 'Physician of the Soul,' " pp. 65–98.

31. Erich Fromm, *Man for Himself. An Inquiry into the Psychology of Ethics*, Holt, Rinehart and Winston, New York, 1947/Routledge and Kegan Paul, London, 1949 (fifth impression, 1967).

32. Erich Fromm, *Psychoanalysis and Religion*, chap. 5: "Is Psychoanalysis a Threat to Religion?" pp. 99–119.

both with genuine religion and with psychoanalysis it is a question of knowledge of the truth, the freedom and independence of man, his capacity for love, of the social conditions in which these things can flourish, of the knowledge of the difference between good and evil, and of listening to one's conscience.

According to Fromm, the attitude—"religious" in the widest sense of the term—of wonder, of rapture, and of becoming one with the universe, is found also in psychoanalysis: a process of breaking through the barriers of the conscious ego and of contact with the hitherto-excluded unconscious, advancing toward a surrender to a framework of orientation which transcends the individual, to an unconditional assent to life. This unconscious, however, is not to be understood either with Freud as the repressed, negative, "evil," or with Jung as practically a source of revelation and a symbol for God. Our unconscious, shaped individually in the system of the passions, is from the very beginning in contact with its environment and reacts to it by affirming or denying; it begins already to realize productively or negatively man's need for roots, identity, effectiveness, and devotion, and therefore it contains at one and the same time the lowest and the highest, the worst and the best, the acceptance and rejection of life, all possible wishes, misgivings, ideas, and insights, which must not be repressed but permeated and integrated with the supreme values of the religions. The unconscious thus becomes the point at which positive human possibilities can be realized.

There is, then, no irreconcilable opposition between psychoanalysis and religion, no threat to genuine, humanitarian religion from psychoanalysis. It depends, of course, on what you mean by religion.[33] Certainly there is a threat to the

33. Ibid.

"scientific-magical" aspect of religion, the unverifiable hypotheses on nature and its creation. But there is no threat to the "experiential" or the "semantic" aspect, religious feeling and devotion and symbolic language in life and customs. Even if a psychoanalyst like Fromm is unable to make any positive statements about God, it is at this very point that psychoanalysis can help toward a new appreciation of the profound wisdom recorded in religion.

Neither is the "ritualistic" aspect of religion directly threatened. It is true that Freud rightly observed a parallelism between certain religious rites and neurotic obsessional actions. But he and a number of psychoanalysts overlooked the fact that, in addition to irrational rites which have a repressive and obsessive character, their neglect leading to fear and feelings of guilt, there are also rational forms of worship which promote life and which, without compulsion, "express our devotion to dominant values by *actions* shared by others."[34] Together with secular rites (forms of greeting, clapping by way of applause, reverence for the dead, etc.), there are also meaningful religious rites:

> A religious ritual of washing can be understood as a meaningful and rational expression of an inner cleansing without any obsessional or irrational component, as a symbolic expression of our wish for inner purity performed as ritual to prepare for an activity requiring full concentration and devotion. In the same way, rituals such as fasting, religious marriage ceremonies, concentration and meditation practices can be entirely rational rituals, in need of no analysis except for the one which leads to an understanding of their intended meaning.[35]

34. Ibid., p. 108.
35. Ibid., p. 109.

According to Fromm, even modern man has a need for ritual, a need which is largely underestimated.

Of course, despite Fromm's positive appreciation of the function of religion in the individual and socio-cultural spheres, one thing must be noticed. Fromm, like Adler, makes no concessions to belief in God as experience of a reality existing independently of man and the world. For him too, at the heart of the question of religion, the ultimate reality is not God, but man. The question raised is about the function of belief in God, not about the reality of God. According to Fromm, what is important is not so much the affirmation or denial of God, of whom we know nothing, but the affirmation or rejection of certain human attitudes. A human attitude, which Fromm would call "religious" in the humanitarian sense, should be developed; instead of deifying things or aspects of the world, there should be an attitude of love and reason. But will not any serious believer in God agree at least with Fromm's rejection of modern idolatry: "It is not only pictures in stone and wood that are idols. Words can become idols; leaders, the state, power, and political groups may also serve. Science and the opinion of one's neighbors can become idols, and God has become an idol for many."[36] Certainly we can agree with Fromm that God too can become an idol. But cannot God be seen differently even by a psychoanalyst?

In this respect Viktor E. Frankl—born in 1905 in Vienna, often described as the founder of a "third Viennese trend in psychotherapy (logotherapy)" and influential especially in the United States—also goes beyond Jung and Fromm. According to him, man is determined, not only by an unconscious instinctual element (Freud) or even an unconscious psychical element (Jung), but also by an unconscious spiritual element

36. Ibid., p. 118.

or an unconscious spirituality. According to Frankl, the psychotherapist in his everyday practice is continually faced with ideological, spiritual questions, which as such must be taken absolutely seriously. They are not to be a priori unmasked as sublimations of the libido (Freud) or interpreted as the impersonal expression of a collective unconscious, as archetypes (Jung). These are questions which are summed up in the question of the meaning of human life, completely neglected by Freud and all too hastily psychologized by Adler and Jung. A cure is possible—that spiritual orientation which man needs for his health and for directing his life—but it cannot come simply from the soul, the "psyche," but only from the spirit, from the "logos." Consequently, religiosity in particular is not to be repressed. Hence Frankl demands a psychotherapy oriented to the spiritual and to the conscious, but unforced, "will to meaning (logos)." Psychoanalysis must advance to existential analysis, secular confession to medical pastoral care, psychotherapy to logotherapy. Frankl too proceeds empirically. In the light of conscience and the existential-analytical interpretations of dreams, with numerous examples from his own practice, he attempts to convince the reader of the reality of an unconscious religiosity and relatedness to God.

Of course, questions arise here as to whether it is possible to argue so quickly from the "facticity" to the "transcendental quality" of conscience, from the voice of conscience to a "transhuman agent," which is even of "a personal nature," and indeed to an "unconscious God."[37] In the light of this religious

---

37. V. E. Frankl, *Der Unbewusste Gott. Psychotherapie und Religion*, 1947, revised and expanded, Munich, 1974, pp. 45–53, 55. (English translation, *The Unconscious God*, Simon and Schuster, New York, 1975/Hodder and Stoughton, London, 1977, pp. 51–58, 60.) Cf. also by the same author, *Ärztliche Seelsorge. Grundlagen der Logotherapie und Existenzanalyse*, 1946, 8th revised edition, Vienna, 1971. (English translation, *The Doctor and the Soul. From Psychotherapy to Logotherapy*, Alfred Knopf, New York, 1955,

position does not Frankl pass judgment too hastily on "irreligi-ous man," who cannot get beyond conscience in its "immanent facticity"?[38] Where Fromm is too detached in his negative psychology (theology?), does Frankl not pursue too ardently his positive theology (psychology?)? And where Freud sees only the instinctual—in fact, the sexual—Frankl sees already the man-ifestation of the spiritual and even the religious.

This much, however, must be granted to Frankl: decades before the sense of futility threatened to become a mass neurosis, he demanded more clearly than any other of the great psychotherapists that psychotherapy should face the spiritual questions, particularly the question of meaning and finally also the question of God, in order not to evade the confrontation with theology.[39]

Meanwhile, however, psychoanalysts even of Freud's school have paid increasing attention to what Jung and Frankl had pointed out at an early stage. In Freud's Vienna before World War I—there, too, a period of "Victorian" prudery—the problem of repressed sexuality was rightly placed at the center of therapeutical efforts. At that time the id needed an intensive analysis. But now the ego is drawing renewed attention to itself. The socio-cultural conditions of most neuroses should not be overlooked.

From the middle of this century the problem of man's *identity* has been in the foreground. In this connection we may

1965/Souvenir Press, London, 1969); *Der Wille zum Sinn*, Bern, Stuttgart and Vienna, 1972. (English translation, *The Will to Meaning. Foundations and Applications of Logotherapy*, New American Library in association with the World Publishing Company, 1969/Souvenir Press, London, 1971.)

38. V. E. Frankl, *Der Unbewusste Gott*, pp. 48–50. (English translation, *The Unconscious God*, pp. 53–55.)

39. This is the approach of others also from the Viennese School: W. Daim, *Umwertung der Psychoanalyse*, Vienna, 1951; I. A. Caruso, *Psychoanalyse und Synthese der Existenz*, Freiburg, 1952; J. Rudin (following Jung more closely), *Psychotherapie und Religion*, Olten, 1960.

refer to Erik Erikson's *Childhood and Society* (1950)[40] and Rollo May's *Man's Search for Himself* (1953).[41] As a result of his own clinical experiences and those of his colleagues, May observed at that time: "The chief problem of people in the middle decade of the twentieth century is *emptiness*."[42] He added: "The human being cannot live in a condition of emptiness for very long: if he is not growing *toward* something, he does not merely stagnate; the pent-up potentialities turn into morbidity and despair, and eventually into destructive activities."[43] "The experience of emptiness . . . generally comes from people's feeling that they are *powerless* to do anything effective about their lives or the world they live in."[44] Some years later—after the student revolts had broken out in force—May could write: "The cultural values by which people had gotten their sense of identity had been wiped away. Our patients were aware of this *before* society at large was, and they did not have the defenses to protect themselves from its disturbing and traumatic consequences."[45]

Does it, in fact, require today the enormous courage of a Freud to oppose a stale sexual morality and sexual prudery? Is it not the spiritual which is repressed today more than the sexual? In addition to repression, is not the control of

40. E. H. Erikson, *Childhood and Society*, New York, 1950, second revised and enlarged edition, W. W. Norton, New York, 1963; the same author, *Identity and the Life Cycle*, New York, 1959; the same author, *Insight and Responsibility*, New York, 1964; the same author, *Identity, Youth and Crisis*, New York, 1968.

41. Rollo May, *The Meaning of Anxiety*, New York, 1950; *Man's Search for Himself*, New York, 1953, W. W. Norton/Souvenir Press, London, 1975; *Love and Will*, W. W. Norton, New York, 1969/Souvenir Press, London, 1970; *Power and Innocence*, New York, 1972.

42. Rollo May, *Man's Search for Himself*, p. 14.

43. Ibid., p. 24.

44. Ibid.

45. Rollo May, *Love and Will*, p. 26.

sexuality—not sufficiently stressed by Freud—also a genuine problem? In our present-day consumer society are not the specific behavior disorders to be found in the comfort-seeking and self-indulgent attitudes and in addictions of all kinds, from cigarettes to drugs? And is it a question today merely of regaining the capacity for enjoyment and achievement, and not rather of regaining a true sense of life and a purpose in life?

No, the typical neurosis of our time is not the repression of sexuality and guilt, but the lack of orientation, of norms, of meaning. Psychotherapists of the most diverse trends today increasingly deplore "the proliferation of the pleasure principle together with the simultaneous neglect and repression of spiritual and religious principles."[46] The whole development is connected to no small degree with the breakdown of religious convictions and the abandonment of religious rites. Do not these things in particular foster man's individuation and self-discovery, as factors of order could they not offer orientation and, by the fostering and guidance of sensitivity and emotionality, could they not contribute to creativity, an extension of awareness, and even to an authentic regression? For a regression wrongly understood, particularly in the religious sphere, can be a disastrous flight: that is, when someone falls back into infantile patterns of behavior which are not appropriate to his present age and his present situation in life. But a regression rightly understood, with the aid of certain religious practices (prayer, worship, examination of conscience, confession), can be supremely helpful for a healthy person and can smooth the path to progression and maturity, inasmuch, that is, as he reexperiences, positively assimilates, and reintegrates into his self-identification what has been forgotten or repressed.

46. E. Wiesenhütter, *Kritik an Freud*, p. 87; cf. the same author, *Therapie der Person*, Stuttgart, 1969.

Is life without religion psychologically possible? Certainly. Freud himself is a proof of this. But we should recall at this point what the psychoanalyst Erik Erikson says:

> The psychopathologist cannot avoid observing that there are millions of people who cannot really afford to be without religion, and whose pride in not having it is that much whistling in the dark. On the other hand, there are millions who seem to derive faith from other than religious dogmas, that is, from fellowship, productive work, social action, scientific pursuit, and artistic creation. And again, there are millions who profess faith, yet in practice mistrust both life and man. With all these in mind, it seems worth while to speculate on the fact that religion through the centuries has served to restore a sense of trust at regular intervals in the form of faith while giving tangible form to a sense of evil which it promises to ban. All religions have in common the periodical childlike surrender to a Provider or providers who dispense earthly fortune as well as spiritual health; the demonstration of one's smallness and dependence through the medium of reduced posture and humble gesture; the admission in prayer and song of misdeeds, of mis-thoughts, and of evil intentions; the admission of inner division and the consequent appeal for inner unification by divine guidance; the need for clearer self-delineation and self-restriction; and finally, the insight that individual trust must become a common faith, individual mistrust a commonly formulated evil, while the individual's need for restoration must become part of the ritual practice of many, and must become a sign of trustworthiness in the community.

Whosoever says he has religion must derive a faith from it which is transmitted to infants in the form of basic trust; whoever claims that he does not need religion must derive such basic faith from elsewhere.[47]

Freud the atheist undoubtedly rejected Christianity in principle. But in practice was he so remote from it? "As you admit, I have done a great deal for love": this is what Freud wrote as early as 1910 to Pastor Oskar Pfister, the only theologian with whom he remained in intellectual contact throughout his life.[48] In Freud's system at that time, however, there was no place for any concept except that of sexually determined love, the all-embracing libido. It was only at the end of his life that Freud discovered nonsexual love.[49] At that point man became for him more than the mechanistically understood system, driven by the ego-instinct and libido, an *homme machine*, basically isolated and egoistic, which he had built up under the influence of Brücke and the early physiologists. Man was now seen as a being essentially related to others, driven by vital instincts demanding unification with others. Life and love belong together and are more deeply rooted than all sexuality.

As late as 1930, in his *Civilisation and Its Discontents*, Freud had described the Christian commandment of love of neighbor as "not reasonable," as "unpsychological" and "impossible to fulfil."[50] Three years later, in view of the darkening world situation with Hitler's seizure of power, in an open letter (not published in Germany), to Alfred Einstein, Freud called for love "without a sexual aim" as an indirect way of opposing war: "There is no need for psycho-analysis to be ashamed to

47. E. H. Erikson, *Identity and the Life Cycle*, pp. 64–65.

48. S. Freud and O. Pfister, *Briefe 1909–1939*, Frankfurt, 1963, p. 33.

49. Cf. E. Fromm, *The Anatomy of Human Destructiveness*, New York, 1973/London, 1974. Appendix, "Freud's Theory of Aggressiveness and Destructiveness", pp. 439–78.

50. S. Freud, *Das Unbehagen in der Kultur* in *Studienausgabe* 9:268. (*Civilisation and Its Discontents*, S.E. 21:143.)

speak of love in this connection, for religion itself uses the same words: 'Thou shalt love thy neighbour as thyself.' "[51]

What Freud admitted here in theory—love of neighbor—he had practiced for a long time, but without knowing why. As early as 1915 he wrote to James Putnam, the Harvard neurologist: "When I ask myself why I have always behaved honourably, ready to spare others and to be kind wherever possible, and why I did not give up being so when I observed that in that way one harms oneself and becomes an anvil because other people are brutal and untrustworthy, then, it is true, I have no answer."[52]

Is there really no answer?

As a believer in God and particularly as a Christian, I *have* an answer to this question. But this would be the theme of another lecture series.

---

51. S. Freud, "Warum Krieg?" in *Studienausgabe* 9:283. ("Why War?" *S.E.* 22:212.)

52. S. Freud, Letter to J. J. Putnam, 8 July 1915, quoted in Ernest Jones, *Sigmund Freud* 2:465.

RELIGION

THE FINAL TABOO?

ON THE REPRESSION OF
RELIGIOUSNESS IN
PSYCHOLOGY, PSYCHIATRY,
AND PSYCHOTHERAPY

5

What I wish to set forth here has to do with pathology in the broadest sense of the word: with the treatment of suffering human beings, whether the illness be of a physical or a spiritual nature. Pathology itself has, as we know, broadened its scope. Initially concerned strictly with pinpointing diseases anatomically, it has learned to take psychosomatic and anthropological aspects into consideration and has even begun to ponder the connections between disease and society in the form of a social pathology. All this informs my discussion, in which I concentrate on the psychological dimensions of disease but also explore—as I rethink the role of religion—anthropological, psychosomatic, and social perspectives on disease. It seems appropriate to me to start with questions of psychiatry and then push forward through psychoanalysis to social psychology and to some of the consequences for medicine in general.

Repression or Explosion of Religiousness?

Is that the question today: *repression* of religiousness? Is that really the question—when there is a new explosion of religiousness, especially in America? Who could overlook the boom of cults, sects, religious groups of all kinds; the new interest in rampant mythology of every derivation; the rekindled search for mysticism, subjectiveness, cosmic consciousness in a hardly comprehensible religious, cosmic, psychological scene? Doesn't all this, rather, testify against the thesis that religiousness is being repressed in our society? *Religiousness* is understood here as religion in the subjective sense, as a devout view of life, attitude toward life, and life style—whereby I am assuming that a genuine religiousness does exist alongside insincere religiosity.

It is no wonder, then, that this new religiousness has become a topic of investigation for psychologists, psychotherapists, and psychiatrists as well. The Committee for Psychiatry and Religion of the American Psychiatric Association has been asked to produce a report on the psychology of these "zealous and cohesive cult-like groups." It will be interesting indeed to hear more about the historical and social context of these new religious movements; to learn more about the psychological needs and life styles of their disciples; and to uncover the internal mechanisms of these groups (their hierarchy, criteria of conviction, and social control), thereby delving into their psychotherapeutic and sociobiological aspects.

This should please Christian theologians, as they, too, have a strong interest in such studies. The findings may give them the means to explain why so many people are fleeing from traditional religious institutions—especially from the large, established churches—to join small, radical, often fanatical religious groups. They might even contribute to pastoral remedies and counterstrategies. After all, shouldn't theologians and psychiatrists work hand in hand on the very same symptoms of illness?

And yet I hesitate. Not because this would not be a profitable undertaking for theology and psychiatry—of course it would! Not because I am not interested in greater cooperation between psychiatrists and psychotherapists on the one hand and theologians and ministers on the other—on the contrary! But rather because a coalition inspired by these understandable interests would be formed too quickly, too superficially, too opportunistically. The foundations of their respective self-conceptions have not yet been clarified. What does this mean?

The traditional pattern of confrontation—psychiatry versus religion—must first be reconsidered. Religiousness is often seen as nothing more than an object of investigation by purportedly neutral, "objective" scientific observers who have already figured out its mechanisms, identified its deficits, and thought of therapeutic strategies. This is reinforced on a subliminal level (including in such studies as the one mentioned above) by the notion that this kind of religiousness is nothing more than pathological deformation; that the diseased or pathological can be clearly distinguished from the healthy or "normal"; and that enlightenment in the name of psychiatry is the order of the day.

Therefore, caution is advisable here—on both sides! Not because enlightenment is not in the interest of theology; not because theologians should be allowed to shirk the task of enlightening the church and society. But rather because those elements of protest, of resistance, and of alternatives to bourgeois banality and one-dimensionality that find expression in new religious currents should not be reduced to a psychopathological syndrome. These phenomena are too important to be resolved diagnostically and explained away in psychotherapy. And far too seldom do psychiatrists constructively confront religiousness—including their own religiousness, or irreligiousness—in their professional (and perhaps also their personal) lives.

I should like to make it clear at the outset that I do not intend to go into certain topics here. First, I do not wish to take sides a priori with any of the numerous schools of psychotherapy that are open to religion or are even religious themselves. (There are more than one hundred psychotherapeutic organizations in the Federal Republic of Germany alone.) Their relationship to academic psychiatry—from the fate analysis of Leopold Szondi, the logotherapy of Viktor Frankl, and the personal psychotherapy of Johanna Herzog-Dürck, to the different variants of the Jungian and Adlerian systems—is one of latent or sometimes blatant tension. Nor am I interested in examining the myriad connections between ministry and psychotherapy, which have found visible expression in the gratifying establishment of a Committee for Psychiatry and Religion in the American Psychiatric Association and a German Society for Pastoral Psychology in 1972 (with divisions for psychoanalysis, clinical training in pastoral counseling, group dynamics and social psychology, and more). Neither do I wish to elaborate upon a well-known distinction formulated by Viktor Frankl, one that is often treated apologetically but should not be ignored: the distinction between healing of the mind (*seelische Heilung*) as the goal of psychiatry and healing of the spirit (*Seelenheil*—a problematic expression!) as the goal of ministry. Medicine focuses on mental health and theology on spiritual health, but both seek to help suffering individuals. A glance at volume 15 of Kindler's *Psychologie des 20. Jahrhunderts* makes it clear even to the nonpsychologist that the dialogue between theology and psychoanalysis has become extraordinarily complex, for instance regarding the great anthropological topics of love, sexuality, guilt, anxiety, conscience, and death. To be sure, this volume also makes it clear that it would be impossible today—in view of the confusing plurality of theological and therapeutic directions—to find "definitions of ministry and psychotherapy that would be ratified on the broadest basis by representatives of both disciplines."[1]

But these are not my central concerns here. Rather, I am interested in the repression of religion by academic psychiatry (including large portions of psychotherapy and psychology) and thus primarily in the significance religion should be accorded by academic psychiatry—not only within a certain group of specialists, but in psychiatry in general, including psychopharmacology, psychotherapy, and sociotherapy. I speak

1. K. Winkler, "Seelsorge und Psychotherapie" in Gion Condrau (ed.), *Transzendenz, Imagination und Kreativität*, vol. 15 of Kindler's *Psychologie des 20. Jahrhunderts* (Zurich, 1979), p. 376.

not as a specialist in psychiatry—as the reader will know—
nor even as an expert in psychiatric ministry. And I most
certainly am not a neoconservative representative of religious
powers and forces interested in preserving institutionalized
religion as an end in itself. I speak as a committed individual
and a Christian, as one who is deeply affected by the many
people who are confused or disturbed and as one who has,
through experience, come to the conviction that religion—
understood and lived correctly—might help.

Am I mistaken in my impression of academic psychiatry:
that religion may occasionally be present as an object of study,
but usually in a negative form? Hardly ever is it seen as a
positive force for health or healing, much less as a subject for
critical self-reflection by psychiatrists. In their professional
lives, in research, and in therapeutic practice religion rarely
plays a constructive role. It is not fundamental to psychiatrists'
conceptions of themselves as psychiatrists. If we choose to rely
on assertions from the initiated, then some psychiatrists are
decidedly antireligious: religion is a neurosis or psychosis, in
any event an illness requiring a cure. Others are perhaps pri-
vately religious, but professionally they leave religion to priests.
Most, however, pay little heed to religion at all. If religion is
not obviously the source of a neurosis or psychosis in a patient
or client (which does not, after all, occur very often), one
politely refrains from asking about it. Why should one anyway?
In comparison to sexuality, religion is a trifling matter.

Evidence for my assertion? Evidence that religiousness plays
a negligible role in psychiatric practice—in contrast to sexuality? Let us take a look at current psychological, psychiatric,
and psychotherapeutic literature. Here are just four examples
of the marginal status of religiousness:

— The twelve volumes of the German *Handbuch der*

Psychologie[2] contains an entire volume on marketing psychology but only a few lines on the psychology of religion.
— The *Comprehensive Textbook of Psychiatry*[3] contains one article by Mortimer Ostow on "Religion and Psychiatry."[4] Aside from two short sections on "Religion and Society" and "Pastoral Counseling," this article discusses religion at great length in the context of obsessive-compulsive neurosis, phobia, hysteria, depression, schizophrenia, and paranoia.
— In the comprehensive new *Handbook of Innovative Psychotherapies*[5] religion—apart from a chapter by Adrian van Kaams on transcendental therapy—is mentioned only twice in passing (in connection with O. Hobart Mowrer's integrity groups and Jesse Lair's mutual-need therapy).
— In a recent two-volume encyclopedia of psychiatry[6] there is, to be sure, an excellent chapter on "Psychiatry and Religion" by Günter Hole, but in some twelve hundred pages there is only one other reference to "religious ideas," and it is listed in the subject index with the telling cross-reference, "see also delusion, religious."

Am I contending too much when I deduce from these and other similar examples that in academic psychiatry, religion is for the most part treated only as a *pathological* or *marginal* phenomenon? And have I, as a theologian, been spoiled, so to speak, by psychoanalysis and its "hermeneutics of suspicion"

2. K. Gottschaldt, Ph. Lersch, F. Sander, and E. Thomae (eds.), *Handbuch der Psychologie*, 12 vols. (Göttingen, 1959–1978).

3. A. M. Freedman, H. I. Kaplan, and B. J. Sadock (eds.), *Comprehensive Textbook of Psychiatry*, 2d edition (Baltimore, 1976).

4. Ibid., 2:52.1.

5. R. J. Corsini (ed.), *Handbook of Innovative Psychotherapies* (New York, 1981).

6. U. H. Peters (ed.), *Psychiatrie*, 2 vols. (Munich, 1980; new edition, Weinheim, 1983) in Kindler's *Psychologie des 20. Jahrhunderts*.

if I permit myself the blunt question: Why hasn't the American Psychiatric Association, which devotes so much anxious attention to the explosion of religiousness in today's society, confronted the problem in its own ranks? Why hasn't it addressed the problem that—apart from particularly obvious and highly pathological phenomena—religion (religion in the subjective sense, that is, religiousness) is of next to no significance for a large number of psychiatrists today?

To be sure, there are also those who think otherwise, and probably in increasing numbers! And

— if I, as a theologian, side with those psychiatrists who believe that religion should neither be eliminated, nor be avoided in treatment, nor be ignored as unimportant, but rather must be taken very seriously;

— if I, along with the American psychiatrist Edgar Draper, for instance, am compelled to see religiousness neith?r as "categorically sick," nor as a foreign object in my own domain, nor as irrelevant, but am rather of the opinion that religious *convictions*, "like *any other aspect* of the patient's intimate, personal life . . . *require psychological understanding*"[7];

— if I then, along with the German psychiatrist Günter Hole, reject "naive identifications on the one hand and helpless or deliberate neglect of religious subjects on the other" in therapeutic practice and am convinced "that the religious element—entirely dependent on the respective personality structure, upbringing, and individual development—can have both positive and negative effects"[8]:

— *then* I will surely not be misunderstood by psychiatrists if

7. E. Draper, "Psychoanalysis and Religion: A Metapsychological Approach to Religious Data" in R. Cox (ed.), *Religious Systems and Psychotherapy* (Springfield, Ill., 1973), p. 371.
8. G. Hole, "Psychiatrie und Religion" in U. H. Peters (ed.), *Psychiatrie*, 2:510.

I, as a theologian, dare to ask this question: Shouldn't psychiatrists in particular, indeed educated people in general, ask whether a phenomenon of repression may not be at work here and whether this repression of religion might not be just as worthy an object of investigation as its explosion in other societal strata and subcultures?

Using Freud against Freud?

Using Freud, then, against Freud? My answer is a decisive yes—and no! And this is a central point. Freud himself wrote in his *History of the Psycho-Analytic Movement* in 1914, "The theory of repression is the corner-stone on which the whole structure of psychoanalysis rests."[9] The term *repression* can be traced back to the earliest beginnings of psychoanalysis. As Freud often emphasized, it followed inevitably from clinical observations of resistance, elicited by a new technique (by which he means the abandonment of hypnosis and the introduction of free association in the treatment of hysteria). This concept has existed, then, for almost one hundred years, particularly in connection with sexuality. But to my knowledge the repression of religiousness has never been systematically investigated in the field of psychiatry.

Today, every "educated person among the scorners of religion" knows that critical theology—in a spirit of self-criticism—has begun to take the objections Freud expounded in his critique of religion seriously. In the sixties and seventies, critical theology began to digest Freud's critique of religion and, in the process, to recognize how many false battles have been fought

9. S. Freud, *Geschichte der psychoanalytischen Bewegung*, quoted in *Studienausgabe* 3:105. See also *Die Verdrängung* and *Das Unbewußte* in *Studienausgabe* 3:103–73. (*On the History of the Psycho-Analytic Movement* in *S.E.* 14 [1957]:16. See also *Repression* and *The Unconscious* in *S.E.* 14:143–215.)

from the very beginning between psychoanalysis and religion, from both sides (with one great exception: the Protestant minister Oskar Pfister of Zurich, the only theologian with whom Freud maintained contact throughout his life).[10] But I do not have the impression that the theological response to Freud's critique of religion has been sufficiently acknowledged by psychiatry, psychotherapy, and especially psychoanalysis. This behooves me to recapitulate here the important points in the critique and response.

Three aspects in a decisive "*with* Freud" are important to me, especially in view of the current exaggerated criticism that misunderstands and rejects psychoanalysis as a rigid and dogmatic system:

First, Freud's criticism was justified, most certainly with reference to the abuse of power by the churches and the superego effect of their moralism and dogmatism through the centuries. Numerous ecclesiogenic neuroses have come from the clerical control of souls in the name of God; the dependency and subjection of poor sinners by repressive confession practices; submission to taboos from untested authority; sexual repression and suppression in ever-changing forms; disregard for women; animosity toward progress and science; and mistaken ideas of good and evil—right up to the present time. Freud's criticism of the traditional authoritarian image of God was especially justified. Behind its ambivalence we see our own infantile father or mother image, projected into the metaphysical realm (the beyond, the future). Often enough, the punishing father-God was, and is, consciously misused by parents as a tool for disciplining children—with long-term ill effects on the religiousness of the young. Also typical of parochial-Catholic socialization is the triad mother image /

10. E. L. Freud and H. Meng (eds.), *S. Freud/O. Pfister: Briefe, 1909–1939* (Frankfurt am Main, 1963).

mother of God / Mother Church, or papalism / Marianism / cel-
ibatism. Finally, Freud was justified in his overall criticism of
any religion, whether Catholic or Protestant, that has lost sight
of reality, binding its followers to a tyrannical superego. Religion has often entailed a return to infantile behavior structures, a regression to childhood wishes, and a substitute
satisfaction by means of a compulsion for cult-like repetition
(comparable, in fact, to the cleanliness compulsion of the obsessive-compulsive neurotic).

Second, Freud was right when he called for honesty in connection with religion, considering all "possible deceits and intellectual naughtiness" (for instance in using the word *God*)
and when he protested in the name of critical rationality
against religious hostility to reason (evident in Protestant biblicism and Catholic traditionalism)—against any "credo quia
absurdum" or moralizing "as-if" philosophy.

Third, there can be no "return to a pre-Freudian state" an-
tedating the discovery of the influence exerted by psychodynamic, unconscious factors—and particularly by the earliest
parent-child relationship (and thus of sexuality in the broadest
sense of the word)—on religion, or, more precisely, on the
image of God and on the distinction between good and evil.
Religion, since that discovery, has also had to submit to psychological analysis. The "test" of psychological explanation
must show how much of my "God" and my religion is merely
a product of my own subconscious. The time has passed when
theologians could speak so simply of the "Lord God"—that all
too human, all-powerful, all-knowing, all-controlling being—
and they should no longer be accused of doing so. Indeed, as
Edgar Draper confirms, the time has passed when institutionalized religion was not "particularly troubled over its bizarre
adherents, wild movements, peculiar saints, lascivious Brah-
mans, paranoid preachers, disturbed rabbis, eccentric bishops,

or psychopathic popes." Traditionally religion "has not seen fit to acknowledge character strengths in those heretics, reformers, or rebels who opposed its teachings. In short, it had not been interested in the personality sources of religious manifestations but rather had stood ready to acclaim hysterical or psychotic phenomena as signals of the Holy Spirit."[11] But a return to such pre-Freudian times is no longer possible.

But what can be said *against* Freud? Here I may well find agreement among many of today's psychoanalysts who are open to criticism and have demonstrated the courage to break new ground.

First, Freud's "hypothesis" of the Oedipus complex as the source of human religion and of the prehistoric killing and eating of a "totem God" has been unmasked by ethnological research on the history of religion. It has proved to be a preconceived notion about religion that reveals less about the ancient history of mankind than about the "tragic secrets of the modern Western intellectual,"[12] who has proclaimed the "death of God" but has not been able to cope with it.

Second, the influence of psychodynamic, unconscious factors and particularly of the parent-child relationship on religion and the image of God can indeed be analyzed psychologically, but, contrary to Freud's assumption, this does not allow any conclusions about the existence of God. The wish for a God ("projection"!) is, of course, not an argument for the existence of God, but neither is it an argument against it; the desire for God can find correspondence in a real God. At the conclusion of his critique of religion, Freud, too, must concede, "We tell

11. E. Draper, *Psychiatry and Pastoral Care* (Philadelphia, 1965; 2d edition, 1970), p. 117.

12. M. Eliade, "Cultural Fashions and the History of Religions" in J. M. Kitagawa (ed.), *The History of Religions: Essays on the Problem of Understanding* (Chicago, 1967), pp. 21–38; quote from p. 25.

ourselves it would be very nice indeed—a moral world order and a life in the hereafter—but it is quite conspicuous that all this is exactly as we must wish it to be."[13] It is conspicuous, to be sure, but that is still not a sound argument against religion.

Third, although psychoanalysis, according to Freud, is "a research method, an impartial tool"[14] unsuitable for constructing an atheistic Weltanschauung, in the end he does use it as a universal instrument of enlightenment (to explain literature and art, mythology, anthropology and education, ancient history, and the history of religion). But the atheistic belief in science propagated by Freud and others has never been able to displace the belief in God—neither in the West nor in the East. Instead, the belief, once so proudly espoused, in a "god Logos," a god of science or progress, is now sorely shaken.

Fourth, Freud's personal atheism was not his original conviction; rather, it was adopted. He did not by any means grow up without religion, as his biographer Edgar Jones mistakenly contends. Even the seven-year-old boy was intensely interested in the Philippson Bible, a bilingual edition (Hebrew and German) of the Old Testament prepared by the Leipzig rabbi Philippson. This was the standard edition of the Holy Scripture read by emancipated Jews in the nineteenth century.[15] Freud, understandably repelled by Catholic ritualism and anti-Semitism and burdened with an Oedipus complex, did not choose the medical profession in order to "help the suffering," but rather out of a "need to understand something of the

13. S. Freud, *Zukunft einer Illusion* in *Studienausgabe* 9:167. (*The Future of an Illusion* in *S.E.* 21 [1961].)

14. Ibid. 9:170. (*S.E.* 21.)

15. See J. vom Scheidt, *Der unbekannte Freud: Neue Interpretationen seiner Träume durch E. H. Erikson, A. Grinstein, H. Politzer, L. Rosenkötter, M. Schur u. a.* (Munich, 1974), pp. 12, 25 ff., 29 f., and 32f.

riddles of the world in which we live and perhaps even to contribute something to their solution."[16] In the process, the ostensibly atheistic-mechanistic natural science of the nineteenth century became a cure-all for life's troubles. In the end, it led Freud the student to become an atheist.

It is certain that a divergence of opinions about sexuality and religion helped turn Freud and his first important associates away from and against each other. Even Alfred Adler and Carl Gustav Jung doubted his idea that the source of all intentions, aside from the instinct for self-preservation, lies in sexual wishes, the libido—even allowing for the more comprehensive Freudian interpretation of "sexual" as a feeling of sensual pleasure. They also doubted that the individual structure of the mind can be understood only retrospectively, in light of past events, instead of equally or even primarily in light of the meaning and goal of life that an individual either determines or adopts. It is true that Adler and Jung left open the question of whether God exists outside of our own consciousness and psyches, but in no way did they reject religion as such. Adler tolerated it benevolently, and Jung took a basically positive stance toward religion in analysis and therapy. In the interest of fairness, though, it must be said that Jung's fascination with the Rosicrucians and his naïveté, persisting into World War II, about the inhumanity of Nazi fascism appear incomprehensible to us today.

It is a strange story, to be sure. At the beginning of the psychoanalytic movement religion was still fought over and argued about. But today? There is a peculiar reservation among many, so that a work as argumentative as *The Future of an Illusion* seems almost like a pastoral stroke of good luck to a

16. S. Freud, "Nachwort zur *Frage der Laienanalyse*" in *Gesammelte Werke* 14:290. ("Postscript to *The Question of Lay Analysis*" in *S.E.* 20 [1959]:253.)

theologian. Hardly thinkable today. (Tilman Moser's *God Poisoning*[17] was the exception—but just that: the exception.) There is no more fighting, neither pro nor contra. There is silence, just as Freud was silent about why he became an atheist, even though he never escaped the question of religion—the religion of his Jewish people—even in the last years of his life. Religion—concealed, forgotten, repressed? Religion—an unconquered zone? Religion—the final taboo?

The Repression of the Oldest, Strongest, Most Urgent Wishes of Humanity

I ask psychiatrists and psychotherapists alike whether it would not be worthwhile to subject *religious defense mechanisms* to an exact scientific, psychological, psychoanalytic, psychiatric investigation. If Freud's own analysis of religious ideas is correct—that is, that religion fulfills the "oldest, strongest, most urgent wishes of humanity" ("illusorily," to be sure, in his opinion)—and if "the secret of their strength is the strength of these wishes,"[18] then their repression must have consequences. And the consequences could be highly destructive.

Substitute fulfillment does not solve the problem but rather aggravates it. A modern form of repression occurs when religious wishes are fulfilled in a "secular" fashion (in such partial spheres as career, family, or political, cultural, social, or athletic activity). When relative values (such as money, career, sex, knowledge, party, or leader) are made formally absolute, we speak of a "cult" or "substitute religion." But are the wishes fulfilled by true religion not the oldest, strongest, most urgent

17. T. Moser, *Gottesvergiftung* (Frankfurt am Main, 1976).
18. S. Freud, *Zukunft einer Illusion* in *Studienausgabe* 9:164. (*The Future of an Illusion* in *S.E.* 21.)

ones for the very reason that they penetrate and comprise all facets of human reality, that they literally transcend human one-dimensionality? Do they not lead to an ultimate and unconditional depth, in short, to the dimension of the absolute? Religion gives life to questions about the meaning of the whole of human existence and world history—and answers them in different ways. These questions cannot be quieted by partial experience through the senses alone. Religion seeks not only a relative fulfillment in the here and now but a definitive fulfillment through the senses in life as well as in death. It seeks not only individual justice but absolute justice for every person. It seeks not only conditional but unconditional standards and norms. It looks toward a final spiritual home, toward an endless horizon, toward an eternal promise.

I do not by any means wish to suggest simple parallels between sexuality and religiousness, much less to assert a symmetry between the two. Religion is a much more complex, but also ambivalent phenomenon; it can be used by the individual for psychopathic, homeostatic, or therapeutic purposes. Thus, in Freudian terms, religion cannot be reduced to its superego function either. Like sexuality, religiousness is surely an expression of elementary id wishes, and at the same time it can motivate and reinforce ego operations with its dogma, norms, and rites. But unlike sexuality, religion makes reference to an entirely different reality, one that can be experienced only through faith, one that both embraces and transcends the human being and his or her world. It does not refer naively to the "Lord God" but rather to the very first, very last, truest reality in all things. This is a reality that cannot be demonstrated by means of rational proof, but it is one we can approach with reasonable trust. And on the basis of that trust we can address it with various (yet always analagous, symbolic, codelike) words.

Whatever recent experimental dream research may have to say to counter the idea that dreams are the disguised fulfillment of repressed wishes, couldn't some (but not all!) of the neuroses of our times and their symptoms be diagnosed as products of spiritual traumata? Because *homo patiens* in modern times no longer admits and embraces his deepest, hidden religious wishes, emotions, affects (similar to the sexual ones), but rather has shifted them to the unconscious by means of a defense mechanism and fixed them there—in short, "repressed" them? This leads either to substitute satisfactions, daydreams, parapraxias, and pathological symptoms or to projection onto substitute objects (persons, ideas, movements) that often take on a fanatical, absolute significance.

And is it possible that therapy for the modern *homo patiens* may succeed only when those previously denied wishes, emotions, and affects are not simply written off but are revealed as subjects of repression, raised into consciousness, and relieved by means of decision—acceptance or rejection? Might the spiritual diseases of our times, then, be healed by uncovering those unconscious, unfinished traumatic experiences and affects that invade our consciousness despite all the resistance it puts up? Could people now, in the postmodern era, gain a new understanding of themselves in all their depth: through insight into the unconscious structures and dynamics at work here; through renewed experience of repressed positive or negative feelings; through discovery, interpretation, and formulation of unconscious motivations and behavioral patterns?

This could possibly lead to a lasting change in the spiritual economy of our postmodern society, and certain pathological symptoms could disappear, so that the *homo patiens* can love and work again in a new way, thus attaining the goal Freud set for every therapy. "I have, as you concede, done much for love," Freud wrote in 1910 to the pastor Oskar Pfister.[19] But at that time his system included only the concept of sexually determined love, the all-encompassing libido. As late as 1930, in his book *Civilisation and Its Discontents*, Freud had characterized the Christian obligation of charity as "unreasonable," "unpsychological," and "unpracticable."[20] It was not until three years later, in the ominous year of 1933, when the National Socialists seized power, that Freud also called for love "without sexual goals" in an open letter (not published in Germany) to Albert Einstein. In an indirect attack on war, he wrote, "There is no need for psycho-analysis to feel ashamed to speak of love in this connection, because religion itself uses the same words: 'Thou shalt love thy neighbour as thyself.' "[21]

Here, if not sooner, it becomes clear (and this is substantiated in the works of such later representatives of the Freudian school as Erik Erikson, Rollo May, and Erich Fromm) that these fears, aggressions, and frustrations—precipitated by a failure to satisfy, to make conscious, to deal with "humanity's oldest, strongest, most urgent wishes"—have far-reaching significance not only for the individual, but also for society. The characteristic neurosis of our times is probably no longer repressed sexuality (what is there left to be repressed?) but rather the *lack of orientation, lack of norms, want of meaning, and emptiness* suffered by countless people. Isn't the whole critical development in modern times—right up to the problem of susceptibility, even among the young, to alcohol, drugs, and criminality on the one hand, and to practical nihilism, terror-

19. *S. Freud/O. Pfister: Briefe*, p. 33.
20. S. Freud, *Das Unbehagen in der Kultur* in *Studienausgabe* 9:191–270. (*Civilisation and Its Discontents* in *S.E.* 21:59–145.)
21. S. Freud, "Warum Krieg?" in *Studienausgabe* 9:283. ("Why War?" in *S.E.* 22:212.)

istic anarchism, and suicide on the other—isn't this development related to the severing of our ethical-religious convictions, norms, and communities? In other words, to what Viktor Frankl diagnosed very early in his meaning-centered "logotherapy" as an "existential vacuum"? It would seem worthwhile, then, to investigate the sociopsychological potency of religion—no matter where that may take us. This point has been made by, among others, the German psychoanalyst and social psychologist Horst Eberhard Richter.[22]

On the Analysis of the God Complex

In *The God Complex* Richter describes modern Western civilization, molded by science, technology, and industry, as a psychosocial disorder. He sees it as a flight from the human powerlessness of the Middle Ages to the claim of egocentric, god-like omnipotence. Drawing on contemporary philosophy and the observation of numerous sociocultural phenomena, Richter traces the path of the anxiety-driven modern individual who has lost his God, but appropriated his power. This, he concludes, has led to excessive demands on man and to a collective impotence-omnipotence complex: the "God complex."

I would like to cite Richter's book here as just one approach to analyzing the psychopathology of modern society, which in its godlessness has forfeited friendship among human beings and with nature. This postmodern criticism of modern spirituality gives us food for thought, with its analysis of the "damaged individual's utopian hopes of salvation" in Marx, Freud, and Marcuse. It confronts squarely the divorce from emotion,

22. H. E. Richter, *Der Gotteskomplex* (Reinbek, 1979). (*All Mighty: A Study of the "God Complex" in Western Man*, trans. Jan Van Heurck, Claremont, Calif., 1984.)

the subjugation of women, the suppression of humanitarianism, the interaction between the psyche and social repression; and finally, above all, the pathological inability to suffer, or "flight from suffering".[23] This flight is expressed concretely in the "denial of suffering" through hysterical overindulgence in our party culture, the "avoidance of suffering" through removal of death from our everyday world, the "appeasement of suffering" through substitute satisfaction in cults of consumption and sex, and the "concealment of suffering" through social techniques and a false mentality of public assistance.

And the *therapy* for overcoming the God complex—is it a question of survival for modern society under the threat of self-destruction? Richter calls, for instance, for an "affirmation of death" and the "attainment of a human balance between powerlessness and omnipotence."[24] He calls for the "ancient phenomenon of sympathy as a foundation for solidarity and justice";[25] he emphasizes compassion and trust. And yet I cannot refrain from asking one question: As correct and important as all this surely is, is it viewed deeply enough and approached radically enough from a therapeutic perspective? It seems very strange that in the therapeutic section of this discourse there is not another word about religion. Nor, for that matter, is it mentioned in Richter's autobiography.[26] Certainly not out of naïveté—but perhaps out of unacknowledged helplessness? Although this therapist contends that the shaken relationship to God requires a long process of painful struggling, in the end he himself seems to evade just that. Religion no longer comes

23. Ibid., pp. 127–87.
24. Ibid., p. 228.
25. Ibid., p. 228.
26. See also H. E. Richter, *Die Chance des Gewissens: Erinnerungen und Assoziationen* (Hamburg, 1986.)

to the fore in therapy; it is a blind spot, a gray, unmastered zone.

Of course, the problem need not be personalized; and Horst Eberhard Richter has (like so many others) doubtless had negative experiences with institutionalized religion. From my own experiences as a theologian, I can certainly respect his hesitancy to speak freely about religion and God. Nevertheless, I ask myself if the spiritual crisis of the times really can be surmounted when the underlying religious dimensions of our human existence are disregarded, when whatever is resting in the deepest depths of humanity is ignored. As much as one may agree with Richter's appeal for "sympathy," the question of *why* one should act this way, and not otherwise, *why* one should be sympathetic, compassionate, and basically human does not enter into the discussion here—nor into other sociopsychological analyses of our day. What is the basis for such a highly ethical attitude? Can sympathy and trust be grounded in biology, in a postulated mother-child relationship that would have to retain its influence throughout an entire life? Can sympathy and trust simply be elevated to universal principles and thus become the foundation of a societal program? Can people be persuaded this way and their attitudes changed? Can mistrust and hate, brutality and ruthlessness—in short, inhumanity—be conquered this way? Why shouldn't I be unreliable, ruthless, and inhumane if that is in my interest; why should I prefer trust to mistrust, sympathy to hate, honesty to lies, benevolence to brutality? The fact that Sigmund Freud himself had no answer to this question should make social psychologists and psychiatrists stop and think. We need to reconsider Freud's troubling remark cited at the close of the first part of this book. "When I ask myself," he wrote, "why I have always behaved honourably, ready to spare others and to be kind wherever possible, and why I did not give up doing so when I observed that in that way one harms oneself and becomes an anvil because other people are brutal and untrustworthy, then, it is true, I have no answer."[27]

No, the answer to the ethical question "Why should I?" is never provided, and since Nietzsche's proclamation of an area "beyond good and evil" Kant's categorical imperative, supposedly instilled in everyone, no longer holds. To be sure, religion cannot answer the question of "Why?" with a pat pronouncement that "God wants it this way" or even "So you will get into heaven." But new reflection on the function of religion is in order, because it is religion, after all, that has both justified and reified the ethos of humanity over the millenia. And the fulfillment of Nietzsche's prediction that nihilism would result from atheism makes such reflection all the more urgent! Sociopsychological analyses such as Richter's offer no answers to questions of values and norms, much less to questions of belief and meaning—meaning even of life's negative experiences: pain, renunciation, failure, sickness, suffering, and death. And these questions—along with the acceptance of our own mortality—have to do with religion, whether affirmed or denied. As impressive as the sociopsychological analyses are, the therapy they offer is inadequate. Here, if not sooner, the limitations of orthodox Freudian psychoanalysis become apparent. Its methodological premises make it difficult for it to transmit values and norms, belief and meaning. A reevaluation of religion as a reality in the sphere of psychiatry presses itself on us, and in light of recent publications and developments it seems in no way inappropriate.

27. S. Freud, Letter to J. J. Putnam, 8 July 1915, quoted in E. Jones, *The Life and Work of Sigmund Freud*, 3 vols. (New York, 1953–1957), 2:418.

On the Treatment of the God Complex

Even at the beginning of our century Albert Schweitzer, in his *Psychiatric Study of Jesus*,[28] identified as a basic methodological mistake the equation of "what is unique and strange to us" with the pathological. And even thirty years ago, the Tübingen psychiatrist Hans Heimann pointed out that distinguishing between "pathologically religious" and "normally religious" phenomena is extraordinarily difficult; conversion, more than any other religious experience, urgently demands "clarification and delineation from the abnormal and diseased."[29] Regarding prophecy and mental illness, Heimann writes that for the Old Testament prophets "both the attitude and the content of their messages were in keeping with the spiritual scope of their work," whereas the pathological reveals itself precisely in the "lack of proportion between the attitude and content of the message and the spiritual world" of the prophet.[30] The religious ideal will probably always deviate from the statistical norm.

On the current hermeneutic level of consciousness, Günter Hole has recently pointed out the limits of objective evaluations of psychological phenomena in religious as well as nonreligious domains. "The subjective standpoint and an inescapable factor of evaluation" are always present,[31] so that such terms as "delusions," "hallucination," "vision," and "ecstasy" but also "guilt," "possession," "glossolalia," and, above all, "conversion" ("rebirth") must be handled with great caution. He, too, em-

---

28. A. Schweitzer, *Die psychiatrische Beurteilung Jesu* (1913; reprint, Tübingen, 1933). (*Psychiatric Study of Jesus*, Boston, 1948.)

29. H. Heimann, *Religion und Psychiatrie* in H. W. Gruhle (ed.), *Psychiatrie der Gegenwart*, vol. 3 (Berlin, 1961), p. 481.

30. H. Heimann, *Prophetie und Geisteskrankheit*, Berner Universitätsschriften 11 (Bern, 1956).

31. G. Hole, "Psychiatrie und Religion," p. 519.

phasizes that a well-founded differentiation is possible only by considering the total context and the pathological detail. And he adds a warning: It is only natural that determining these boundaries of the pathological is particularly difficult for psychiatrists who have no personal experience of religious conviction or behavior and who thus can hardly draw any conclusions by analogy to their own spiritual life, as they otherwise usually would.

Considering the historical origins of modern experimental psychology in the mid-nineteenth century, it is easy to understand why little attention was given to religion; why psychology was dealt with only on a physiological-biological basis; why it did well to emancipate itself from the prevailing speculative philosophy and psychology of classical and Christian origin; why it was tested in research and training laboratories, powerfully stimulated by quantification and, at first, strongly influenced by the philosophical doctrine of critical empiricism and materialism. But it should not be forgotten that even those two giants of early experimental psychology, Wilhelm Wundt and William James, studied the psychology of religion intensively with the (at least subjectively real!) "varieties of religious experience"—as did the great founders of modern sociology, Max Weber and Émile Durkheim. Later psychologists, psychotherapists, and psychiatrists were perplexed by religion, because their instruments of knowledge, developed in the natural sciences, were hardly suited to the investigation of religious phenomena.

I certainly don't want to draw a caricature of psychiatry in the spirit of a theologically motivated "antipsychiatry." Today some have begun to distinguish more clearly between profit and loss in the *exclusive* application of the logic of natural science to the humanities. It has become more clear that all the measuring, experimenting, and extrapolating of the highly

developed behavioral sciences—as terribly important as it is—
rests on a preliminary understanding of human reality that
encompasses only certain aspects and dimensions of it. In any
case, the ancient and perpetually new questions about the
meaning of human life and action, about the standards of
human behavior and about the value of the individual and
society have become, as we have seen, anything but superfluous. Empirical and humanistic theories and methods should
therefore be combined more often, particularly because, as
Rollo May puts it, "our science can indeed test some values,
but the *content* of these values is not derived from it."[32] More
and more psychiatrists are beginning to understand that, even
though they may be able to help their psychotic patients for a
limited time (with psychotropic drugs, for instance), they are
still far from understanding the true nature of the conflicts
and reductions of the postmodern individual.

It is heartening to see that the boundaries between the various schools of psychotherapy, once so clear, have become in-
distinct today in many cases; correction and supplementation
by other methods of healing are in great demand. In addition
to psychoanalysis and behavior therapy, humanistic therapy,
under the aegis of Abraham Maslow, Charlotte Bühler, and
Carl Rogers, has established itself as the "third force."[33] The
one-sidedness of the other two methods—in particular the
retrospective pessimism of psychoanalysis and the atomistic
reductionism of behaviorism—are being avoided more and
more through concentration on the experience of the whole,

32. R. May, *Antwort auf die Angst* (Stuttgart, 1982), p. 231. (*Psychology and
the Human Dilemma*, New York, 1967.)
33. For an informative overview of the three main trends in psychotherapy,
see D. Revenstorf, *Psychotherapeutische Verfahren*, vols. 1–3; volume 4 discusses
group, pair, and family therapy (Stuttgart, 1982–85).

unreduced person, on specifically human existence as well on positive forces, on meaningfulness and dignity. Shouldn't the quite unorthodox representatives of current psychotherapy, such as Ruth Cohn, Karlfried Graf Dürckheim, or Leopold Szondi, also be considered here without any partisanship? Szondi, for example, has provided an acute analysis of the differences not only between belief and delusion, but also between the ability to believe and disturbances in belief.

Keeping this panorama in mind, it seems to me that those more recent developments in the field of psychotherapy which assign a positive function to religiousness should also be understood and taken seriously in academic psychiatry—not just as peripheral phenomena, but as manifestations that are symptomatic of our times. The following movements seem important to me for any desirable, comprehensive theory and therapy that attempts to integrate findings from various methods:

1. For decades, thousands of *self-help groups* like Alcoholics Anonymous (AA)—inspired, incidentally, indirectly by C. G. Jung—but also Gamblers Anonymous (GA), Overeaters Anonymous (OA) or Emotions Anonymous (EA) have worked, often successfully, on severe mental disturbances hardly accessible to conventional therapies.[34] Many of these groups are founded on the conviction that such individuals can no longer cope with their life situations alone and that it is helpful for them to acknowledge a divine power "outside" themselves. This power, which is larger than they are (however the individual may understand this), gives them new confidence and courage for a fearless inventory of their lives, gives them the courage to ask for help toward self-help and for forgiveness of guilt.

---

34. See *Alcoholics Anonymous*, 3d edition (New York, 1976) and *Alcoholics Anonymous: A Brief History of AA* (New York, 1957).

2. Jesse Lair's *mutual need therapy*[35] is an attempt to apply the dynamics of the "twelve-step treatment program" of Alcoholics Anonymous to non-abusers in order to include not only the physical-somatic and the intellectual-mental, but also the spiritual dimension (for instance through prayer and meditation) in order to bring about fundamental attitude change and personality reorganization.

3. O. Hobart Mowrer's *integrity groups*,[36] also inspired by Alcoholics Anonymous, work on the basic assumption that such symptoms as anxiety, guilt, and self-alienation—so prevalent in our modern industrial society—can be viewed as entirely adequate reactions to the destruction of personal integrity (dishonesty, lack of responsibility, failure in interpersonal relations); that these are behaviors more than emotions, "socioses" more than neuroses, and are characterized not by "oversocialization," as Freud's theory of the superego assumes, but rather by "undersocialization," resulting necessarily in an identity crisis. Where family, community, school, and church largely fail, Mowrer thinks, people can still be helped by small group communities in which the participant can practice honesty, responsibility, and sympathy and can go beyond mere conversation to achieve more open and honest interaction with fellow human beings, thus developing a sense of integrity and identity, care for others, and community.

4. In the *transcendental therapy* developed by Adrian van Kaam[37] we find what is addressed more implicitly in all the

35. J. Lair, "Mutual Need Therapy" in R. J. Corsini (ed.), *Handbook of Innovative Psychotherapies*, vol. 1.

36. See A. J. Vattano, "Integrity Groups" in *Handbook of Innovative Psychotherapies*, vol. 1.

37. A. van Kaam, "Transcendence Therapy" in *Handbook of Innovative Psychotherapies*, vol. 1.

other groups by means of their diagnostic and therapeutic methods. Van Kaam is interested not in the treatment of severe neurotic or psychotic disorders, but rather in those problems—inherent to different phases of life—which require the transcendence of a previous life style in favor of a new life form: in crises of separation, direction, continuity, and decision or of life ideals, such as in the midlife crisis. In this therapeutic approach with highly reflected methods—and in contrast to many other therapy forms—repressed spiritual, religious (or humanistic) traditions are also considered; "culturally based anger" must be reduced, so that traditional sources and forms can be rediscovered (for instance through the intelligent use of "bibliotherapy" with classical or modern spiritual texts).

I could continue with this list and include ideas—not yet fully matured, to be sure—that lead some authors, following Abraham Maslow, to speak of a "transpersonal psychology and therapy."[38] Under the influence of Far Eastern methods or of meditative self-encounter, a broadening of consciousness even beyond the limits of the ego and the personality is assumed, so as to attain an optimum of psychological health.

But let us stop here—what fundamental idea has guided our path of reflection? I answer summarily: instead of repression, the reciprocal challenge of religion and psychiatry.

Consequences for a Humane Therapy

In confronting Freud we have recognized what invaluable enlightenment psychiatry has provided into misrepresentations and distortions, neurotic deformations and pathological deficits in the domain of theology, church, and Christianity. The-

38. R. N. Walsh and F. Vaugham (eds.), *Beyond Ego* (Los Angeles, 1980).

ologians and hierarchists, above all, have often enough ignored, waved aside, or apologetically discounted psychiatry's interest in their work so as to immunize the "believers" and the "credulous": anxious self-protection against disruption "from without" has led to the *repression of psychiatry*. And yet it should not be overlooked that after 1945 some theologians and pastoral psychologists recognized clearly the challenge of psychiatry and drew upon the instruments of psychoanalysis for religious-theological illumination.

Corresponding to this process of repression on the part of religion—and this is my thesis—has been an equally severe and deep-seated process of repression within psychiatry: the *repression of religion* in psychiatric theory and practice, where there has been often so little to say in answer to such highly existential questions as belief and disbelief, good and evil, freedom and love, guilt and atonement, meaning and happiness because the "personality" was totally dissolved into processes, the "spirit" was scorned as a philosophical phenomenon, and communication with philosophical anthropology and theology was halted. As a theologian, however, I must acknowledge that the state of discussion within psychiatry today is marked by gratifying changes. Right in the middle of the much-cited "crisis of diagnostics," internal corrections are being made of onesidedness and narrowness, of exclusivity and narcissism—of psychoanalysis on the one hand and behavior therapy on the other. The influence of a humanistic psychotherapy that gives simultaneous consideration to somatic, psychological, and social aspects and that tries to integrate them in a comprehensive anthropology has doubtless created a new climate for dialogue between psychiatry and religion, new foundations for cooperative efforts. In the new forms of therapy and the tendencies to a more holistic view, religion has assumed quite a positive value. This can be deduced from many symptoms in today's society—and the "explosion of religiousness" cited at the outset should be seen in this context. *Previously repressed topics are reemerging, but in a new form,* in a new, prospective, "postmodern" framework rather than a regressive-medieval paradigm of society in general.

Reciprocal challenge: What do theologians expect of psychiatrists? Certainly not that psychiatrists and psychotherapists play spiritual adviser to their patients, espousing highest values and final standards, attempting to force upon them the knowledge of an absolute meaning, or making themselves the agents of a specific religion or church. As I said at the outset, I am not concerned with the preservation of institutionalized religion as an end in itself; I am concerned first and foremost with the disturbed and troubled people involved, and with the meaning of religion particularly for them. Not for *God's sake,* who truly doesn't need it, but for the *people's sake* do I plead against the repression of religiousness, so that they may remain or may once again become psychologically and physically healthy.

For this reason I am decidedly of the opinion that questions of religion, for the sake of the people—both the sick and the · healthy—cannot be domesticated and relegated to a quasi-illegal garret existence in the great edifice of psychiatry, but rather that they should be included throughout as central questions of psychiatry, psychotherapy, and psychology. I plead not for a religious psychotherapy or a psychotherapy only for the religious, but rather for a therapy that takes the phenomenon of religion seriously as one of the specifically human forms of expression. I plead for a therapy that does not merely take note of the patient's confession of faith or denomination or inquire perfunctorily into his or her orthodox beliefs. Rather, therapy should try to explore in detail an individual's very personal, often very unorthodox religion, which usually undergoes great changes in the course of a lifetime: the patient's "heart religion."

The psychotherapist Edgar Draper, quoted at the outset, considers some knowledge of this undisguised personal philosophy of life to be a psychological *via regia* toward understanding a particular person: "Very simply, then, if one can learn what specific tenets or religion are of importance to a person at any one particular time in his life, one can learn of his current crisis, his struggles of development, his character structure, and make accurate clinical and psychodynamic diagnoses."[39]

For patients it cannot be a matter of indifference whether their psychiatrists understand something about religion (about genuine, healthy, true religion, of course); whether they have a feel for the spiritual sources of power that reside in religion; whether they can lead their patients to such sources—possibly buried within them—which may then be more healing, integrating, and constructive than pure analysis. A person who, owing to a lack of receptivity or education, has no experience of music, will never be able to evaluate accurately the healing or inspiring power of music. This person is poorer than others. Likewise, the person who has not come to know religion (be it owing to personal barriers, philosophical premises, or societal prejudices) will never know the great spiritual resources that can be decisive for the well-being of a patient. This person is poorer than those who have experienced religion in an emancipating, healing sense.

Let there be no misunderstandings. I am not saying that all the problems of our times can readily be solved by a new religiousness. I am far too conscious of the enormous com-

39. E. Draper, "Psychoanalysis and Religion," p. 373.

plexity of the situation to make such a pronouncement. It is clear to me, as I stated at the beginning, that many problems of our times exist precisely because people have adopted a false religiousness. But as I see it, it is the Christian theologian's task to bring forward criteria for distinguishing critically between true and false religiousness.

And what should these criteria be? "Surely Christian criteria," I might say here as a Christian theologian, and I have said that often enough. But, if possible, I would like to speak here for non-Christians as well, and thus I use an inclusive formulation. True religiousness exists wherever religion—in the interest of psychological or social health (for example, in Latin America, South Africa, or the Philippines)—works not to enslave but to emancipate; not to injure but to heal; not to destabilize but to heal. True religiousness exists wherever religion is a basis for a true realization of the self and for a goal-oriented mastery of personal as well as societal challenges.

Yes, I believe that our basic outlook will have to change if humanity is to survive: we will have to adopt a truly humane outlook. Theoretically, this can be achieved without religion, through an atheist or agnostic approach—let us not debate that point—but without religion it will lack an unshakable, unconditional, and universal foundation.

It is the task of the theologian—really, of every religious person—to combat all pathological distortions in favor of genuine, healthy, true religiousness and religion. We should work for a religion

— that supports self-acceptance without regression;
— that can serve the individuation of the individual with its symbols, convictions, and rites;
— that can once again provide spiritual guidance and ethical standards, especially to our younger generation;

— that, though fully aware of the limits of free will and culpability, guarantees freedom of decision, identity, and dignity, through all behaviors and processes of learning;
— that is able to conquer fears and to justify trust, understanding, and respect—the basis for friendship and love;
— that encourages and guides sensitivity and emotionality, thus promoting creativity, the expansion of consciousness, and more humanity among human beings.

True humanity is the presupposition of true religion. This means that the *humanum*, or respect for human dignity and fundamental values, is a minimal demand made on every religion. There must be at least humaneness (this is a minimal criterion) wherever one wishes to realize genuine religiousness. And true religion can be the fulfillment of true humanity. This means that religion, as the expression of an encompassing meaning, the highest values, and unconditional obligation, is an optimal presupposition for the realization of the *humanum*. There must be religion (this is a maximal criterion) wherever one wishes to realize humaneness unconditionally and universally.

POSTSCRIPT

Only after the Washington address did I become aware of an important article that had just appeared in the *American Journal of Psychiatry* (March 1986, pp. 329–34), an article I believe strengthens my own theses. Five American psychiatrists (D. B. Larson, E. M. Pattison, D. G. Blazer, A. R. Omran, and B. H. Kaplan) investigated four representative psychiatric journals in the U.S.A., Canada, and Great Britain from the years 1978–1982 to see what sort of role religion played in them. Their interesting observations can be summarized as follows:

1. There is a considerable discrepancy between the religious convictions of psychiatrists and psychologists and of the general public. According to empirical studies, more than 90 percent of all Americans surveyed believe in God, more than 40 percent attend church services once or more a week, and more than 20 percent consider religion to be an important part of their lives. By contrast, only 43 percent of the members of the American Psychiatric Association believe in God, and only 5 percent of the members of the American Psychological Association.

2. The negative attitude of many psychiatrists comes from the psychoanalytic realm and is predicated on Freud's theory of religion, even though it has been criticized as "imprecise and conceptually reductive."

3. Most clinical psychiatric literature has been concentrated on the psychopathological and neurotic practice of religion among psychiatric patients.

4. In comparison to the population as a whole, a substantial number of psychotherapists follow the so-called religious apostasy model. Religious apostates are those who have grown up

in religious homes but now profess to be atheist, agnostic, or without belief. Out of more than three thousand professional psychotherapists, nine hundred (20 percent) had become apostates. Psychoanalysts have the highest apostasy rate (40 percent), in comparison to 26 percent among non-psychoanalytic psychiatrists, clinical psychologists, and psychiatric social workers.

5. All this means that there is a basic discrepancy between the two "populations" in their perception of religion: the general public seem to value religion as a significant factor in their lives, whereas, in general, professional psychotherapists do not. To the public, psychotherapists appear ignorant in matters of religion, or at least rejecting in terms of their own lives, whereas many psychiatrists look down on the religious public as naive, neurotic, or uneducated. The two groups, then, base their understanding of religion on different principles and possess inadequate or distorted information about the religious knowledge of the other group.

6. The quality of the articles in the psychiatric journals that were studied left much to be desired. Not only was the rate of quantitative studies with at least one religious variable low; not only was the conceptualization of psychiatric research into religion inadequate—but especially striking was the ignorance displayed of contemporary research into religious matters. It is sobering to realize that the latest psychiatric research into religion is not on a par with comparable investigations in other behavioral sciences (such as psychology and sociology). Quantitative psychiatric research concerned with religiousness is relatively infrequent in comparison to other behavioral sciences, uses methodologically inadequate instruments, and fails to make suitable use of contemporary conceptual principles from theological research.

7. Psychiatrists' personal evaluation of religion can have a substantial impact on their basis of knowledge. If psychiatrists do not value religion personally, they may conclude that acquaintance with religion in general, and among their patients in particular, is irrelevant. As the authors conclude, the clinical practice of psychiatry is ill-served by the current inadequacies of psychiatric literature. Psychiatrists who lack religious convictions or are ambivalent in their beliefs may receive confirmation from this psychiatric literature that it is irrelevant to know anything about religion. This may lead them to misinterpret the religious dynamics—whether they be healthy or unhealthy—of their patients' lives. The authors close with a quotation from the *Chronicle of Higher Education* (52), which I can only second: "The academic study of religion is not the practice of religion. . . . Religion has always been there, informing our self-understanding, our values, and our public life. It will always be there. The question is whether we will remain vulnerable to its abuse or will acquire the fundamental knowledge and skills to evaluate it."

INDEX

Adler, Alfred, 26, 55, 56–58, 60, 111, 129, 139; views on religion, 61–63, 66, 139

Aggression, 61. *See also* Death-instinct

Alcohol, 143

Alcoholics Anonymous (AA), 151, 152

American Journal of Psychiatry, 159

American Psychiatric Association, 133, 159; Committee for Psychiatry and Religion, 128, 130

American Psychological Association, 159

Analytical psychology (Jung), 59–60

Animal phobias, development of, 37

Animatism, 34

Animism, 33–34, 67, 68

Anthropology: applied to history of religion, 32, 71–72

Anti-Semitism, 10, 11–12, 17, 138

Apostates, 159–60

Atheism, 138; Büchner's influence on, 5; effect of medical studies on, 6; Feuerbach's influence on, 3, 75, 76, 81; of Freud, 7, 15, 75–76, 80, 81, 85–87, 121, 138–40; Marxist, 3, 6, 75–76, 81, 93; materialistic, 6–7; Nietzsche on, 147

Behavior therapy, 150

Belief, religious, 42–44, 50–51, 77; relation to reason, 94, 95–96, 97, 136, 141; repression of, 84–85, 87, 118–19. *See also* Religion

Benedict, Ruth, 72

Bernays, Martha, 17

Bible: influence on Freud's youth, 8–9, 138

Blazer, D. G., 159

Bleuler, Eugen, 26, 55

Boas, Franz, 73

Breuer, Josef, 18, 20

Brücke, Ernst Wilhelm von, 12, 13, 15, 17, 19

Büchner, Ludwig, 3, 5, 7

Bühler, Charlotte, 150

Castration complex, 106–07

Catharsis, method of, 18, 19

Catholicism, 135–36; anti-Semitism of, 11–12, 138; ritualism of, 10–11, 138

Charcot, Jean Martin, 17

Childhood: animal phobias in, 37; innate dispositions vs. experience during, 104–05; relation of religion to, 136; sexuality in, 24–25

Christianity, 153, 157; Freud's aversion to, 11–12, 135–36, 138–39; interpretation of God in, 63; psychological basis of, 39–40. *See also* Catholicism

Churches, 128, 153; misuse of power by, 97–98, 135

Civilisation and Its Discontents (Freud), 42, 121, 143

Cocaine, 17

Cohn, Ruth, 151

Committee for Psychiatry and Religion of the American Psychiatric Association, 128, 130

Communion: relation to totem meal, 39

Community feeling, 58

Complex psychology, 59–60

Comprehensive Textbook of Psychiatry, 132

Comte, Auguste, 33, 35

Conscious, the, 21, 99, 100, 142

Conservation of energy, law of, 13, 59

Conversion, 148

Copernicus, Nicolaus, 3

Counter-transference, 22

Criminality, 143

Cults, 127, 128, 140, 145

Culture, importance of religion in, 45, 47–48

Darwin, Charles, 32, 38

Darwinian theory. *See* Evolutionary theory

Death, 145; Freud's struggle with, 88–89